"Oh, what glories we discover not just in our God's abilities but even in his perfect 'cannots'. Enough indeed to help us know true safety—and sleep soundly. I pray that God will be pleased to expand and deepen and strengthen your vision of him in his precious cannots, and also draw dazzlingly close to you in love when you see what further excellencies he added in Christ."

DAVID MATHIS, Senior Teacher and Executive Editor, desiringGod.org; Pastor, Cities Church, Saint Paul, Minnesota; Author, *Habits of Grace*

"*12 Things God Can't Do* is a wonderful example of why theology matters, why orthodox theology matters, and why having gifted theological teachers matters. The weightiness of content that we so desperately need to nourish us, sustain us, and, yes, help us sleep(!) is balanced by Nick's lightness of touch and pastoral sensitivity. The result is theological exposition that is both relevant and richly affective. Highly recommended."

DAN STRANGE, Director, Crosslands Forum; Author, *Making Faith Magnetic*

"Finally, a book that prides itself on putting you to sleep! *12 Things God Can't Do* is deeply peace-bringing and faith-building. Nick Tucker has an extraordinary gift for making profound truths about the nature of God accessible for ordinary people. This book will give you a greater understanding of the God of the universe and leave you captivated afresh by his perfect character. I wholeheartedly commend it to you."

PHIL KNOX, Head of Mission to Yo[...] Alliance; Author, *Story Bearer*

D1446020

"This is a beautiful book that simultaneously blows your mind and warms your heart! Each chapter creatively and biblically reveals something awesome about God, exploring the Creator/creature distinction to draw the reader into a greater understanding of his character and nature. This book will change you—how you live and how you love. With the turn of each page, your trust in God will grow, and your love for him will increase as you gaze upon his majesty."

MEL LACY, Executive Director, Growing Young Disciples

"*12 Things God Can't Do* fed my soul and blessed my heart in more ways than I could have imagined. By focusing our minds on the very things God can't do, Nick Tucker shows how Scripture speaks to reassure us and to renew a living faith. God really is not like us, and because of that, we find rest for our souls and even more reason to rejoice in our Maker. I can't think of a believer who would not be hugely rewarded by a careful reading of this excellent book."

NEIL POWELL, Pastor, City Church Birmingham

"This beguiling book is more important than its modest size would suggest and has a TARDIS-like quality. The whimsical title will draw you into what becomes a much bigger, more encompassing and more significant journey. It offers a reliable and engaging crash course in apologetics, but then takes you on a breathtaking tour of the doctrines of God, of Jesus and of our humanity, and grips these vital truths in a fascinating theological/historical/philosophical framework. It is a book that improves its readers by not simply teaching us how to think properly but showing how thinking properly about God is foundational to understanding our own identity and how to serve, love and enjoy the one for whom we were made. Everyone should read this."

RICHARD CUNNINGHAM, Director, UCCF: The Christian Unions

"This book is an astonishing achievement. One of the most daunting subjects for the Christian is understanding something of the nature of the triune God. Christians throughout the ages have wrestled with questions like: *Does God really know everything, and, if so, what does that do to free will? Can God change his mind? Does God suffer?* Nick Tucker tackles twelve of the most complex questions people have asked about God and addresses them in a way that is biblically faithful and informed by the best minds in Christian tradition. Rich in theological truths and brimming with helpful illustrations, this is a book that I will recommend to anyone wanting to know God more deeply. I only wish this book had been in print when I was younger!"

SEULGI L. BYUN, Chair and Associate Professor, Department of Biblical and Religious Studies and Philosophy, Grove City College

"I strongly commend this work. We need books on the great teachings of the Bible in an accessible format. Dr Tucker gives us an introduction to Christian beliefs about God which is engaging, clear and applied. I hope that it is widely used in churches."

PETER JENSEN, Former Archbishop of Sydney; Former Principal of Moore Theological College

12 THINGS GOD CAN'T DO

NICK TUCKER

In memoriam
Michael John Ovey

CONTENTS

INTRODUCTION

"**Y**ou're in trouble."

I wasn't sure whether to believe her. Bitter experience has taught me that when someone tells me that I'm in trouble, I probably am. Yet a twinkle in her eye suggested that all was not entirely lost.

"Oh dear," I said, "was it something I said?" (It normally is.)

"I nearly didn't get here this morning," she replied, at which point my heart rate dropped a bit. I was the guest preacher for a church weekend retreat, and I felt pretty sure that this member's transport problems were unlikely to be my fault.

"It's your fault," she added.

"Oh, I'm sorry to hear that…" I had to know more.

It turns out that this lady had lost her husband several years ago. She had not slept through a single night since. That morning, though, she had not lain awake listening to the dawn chorus for hours as usual, but had woken to the sound of banging at her front door, which she eventually realised was the person who had come to drive her to

11

that day's meetings. She had not only slept through the night—she had overslept.

How, you might ask, could this have been my fault? She put her sleepiness down to the talks I had given the evening before. It's not unheard of for my talks to put people to sleep, but normally they wake up when I stop speaking. This time, though, was different. This time, the effect was (to my surprise, I'll admit) exactly what the title of the talk suggested should happen: *12 Things God Can't Do and How They Can Help You Sleep at Night.*

As you read this book of the same title, I'm hoping that you might have a similar experience. Knowing God better really should help us to sleep more soundly.

Don't believe me? Ask King David.

Psalm 3 begins with him describing a situation of appalling stress: "LORD, how many are my foes! How many rise up against me!" (v 1). It's so bad that the talk of the town is that "God will not deliver him" (v 2). David wrote this psalm whilst on the run from his son Absalom, who had led an apparently successful *coup d'état* to take the throne (see 2 Samuel 15 – 18). David escaped, but now had a target on his back.

But Psalm 3 holds a remarkable surprise: "I lie down and sleep; I wake again, because the LORD sustains me" (v 5). To David, the amazing bit of that verse was probably the middle portion: "I wake again". After all, there were plenty of people trying to prevent that outcome.

For me though, I can't get over the fact that he *slept* at all.

Sleep is something we can normally only do when we feel safe. Apparently, on the first night in a new place, half your brain remains alert all night, vigilant to threats.[1] When you think about it, you realise what an act of trust falling asleep normally is. You are so vulnerable: you have no idea what's going on around you and you cannot look after yourself. When we face stress or threats, our bodies' "fight or flight" mechanisms make restful sleep feel like unicorn tears: hard to imagine and impossible to obtain.

So, if people are literally out for your blood, as they were for David's, sleep won't come easily. A soldier in enemy territory won't just lie down and sleep because it's bedtime. Only the watchful eye of a comrade keeping lookout makes sleeping a vaguely safe thing to do. But David slept through this period of terrible stress because he had someone better than a comrade watching over him: "You, LORD, are a shield around me" (v 3). Safe in that knowledge, David says that he will "not fear though tens of thousands assail me on every side" (v 6). As the very next psalm puts it: "In peace I will lie down and sleep, for you alone, LORD, make me dwell in safety" (Psalm 4:8).

---

1 "Night Watch in One Brain Hemisphere during Sleep Associated with the First-Night Effect in Humans", https://www.cell.com/current-biology/fulltext/S0960-9822(16)30174-9 (accessed 4 Oct 2021).

David knew just how powerful God is, and how faithful he is to his promises. And this book aims to give you the same confidence. I long to give you a glimpse of God's greatness that will change the way you see the world—and, yes, help you to sleep at night.

To think about God's greatness, we naturally tend to talk about what God *can* do. We, however, are going to consider twelve things that God *can't* do—and when you realise what God can't do, his greatness might just blow your mind.

To show you what I mean—and while we are on the subject of sleep—consider this: God can't sleep. That's a truth we find in Psalm 121. It's part of a series of psalms called the *Songs of Ascent* which were sung by pilgrims on the challenging, dangerous (and uphill) journey to Jerusalem. As they walked, they sang songs of praise to God to encourage and comfort each other:

> *He will not let your foot slip—*
>   *he who watches over you will not slumber;*
> *indeed, he who watches over Israel*
>   *will neither slumber nor sleep. (v 3-4)*

God will never take his eye off the ball; he will never drift off and fail to watch over and take care of his people. His people can rest, because he won't. Victor Hugo, the author of *Les Misérables*, expressed the point beautifully:

> *Have courage for the great sorrows of life and patience for the small ones; and when you have laboriously*

accomplished your daily task, go to sleep in peace. God is awake.[2]

We sleep because we need to sleep. But God doesn't. And that is an example of a truth that is going to underpin the rest of this book: God is not like us. If we can begin to grasp this, everything in the pages that follow will make a lot more sense.

We tend to see things from our own point of view. So, we often think about God as basically like us, just much, much, bigger. But one of the main things that God wants us to know is that he is not like anything in creation and we shouldn't think of him as if he were. Hence we sleep, but he doesn't.

One of my favourite passages in the whole Bible is Isaiah 40. It begins with an announcement that God is coming to rescue his people (v 1-5). But Israel's immediate circumstances look dire, and are about to get a whole lot worse. How can they be sure that rescue is coming?

See, the Sovereign LORD comes with power,
  and he rules with a mighty arm.
See, his reward is with him,
  and his recompense accompanies him.
He tends his flock like a shepherd:
  he gathers the lambs in his arms

---

2 Victor Hugo, "To Savinien Lapointe. March, 1841" in *The Letters of Victor Hugo: From Exile, and After the Fall of the Empire*, ed. Paul Meurice (Houghton, Mifflin and Company, 1898), p 23.

and carries them close to his heart;
  he gently leads those that have young.

  (Isaiah 40:10-11)

Then, to help us to see how powerful this God who rules with his "mighty arm" really is, Isaiah asks, "Who has measured the waters in the hollow of his hand, or with the breadth of his hand marked off the heavens?" (v 12). The answer to Isaiah's question is obvious: it's only God who can do this. He is uniquely able to do whatever he wants to do. Once you get a sense of what is at the end of God's arm—a hand that can contain all the water in the universe—you don't really need to worry that he won't be able to save you.

This question-and-answer pattern is a device that Isaiah uses several times in chapter 40. If you have time, it's worth reading the whole of Isaiah 40 and asking as you do, "What is God like?" Why not do that now, before you read on? So, what is the God of Isaiah 40 like? You might say that he's strong and wise and good and inexhaustible, and you would be entirely right. But the answer Isaiah repeatedly gives to the question "What is God like?" is "He's like no one else". Time and again Isaiah drives the point home with questions that have the answer "no one"! "Whom did the LORD consult?" (v 14). No one. "With whom ... will you compare God?" (v 18). No one. "Who is [his] equal?" (v 25). No one. You get the point: God is incomparable.

He is incomparable in terms of scale; the universe is small enough relative to him that he can measure the heavens with the span of his hand and weigh the dust of the earth on a little set of scales. He is incomparable in terms of knowledge; no one has ever had to teach him anything. He is also incomparably holy.

For the Israelites in the Old Testament, the sacrificial system in the temple served as a visible reminder of God's holiness. Animals were killed and burned on the altar on a daily basis. The message was clear: to come near to a holy God was a serious, costly, bloody business. Isaiah takes that image and puts it on steroids. He takes Lebanon—a place famous for its enormous cedar trees—and says, *Imagine you cut down all the trees in Lebanon and piled them on top of each other to make an altar fire to God.* It would be an inferno like none the world has ever seen. *But*, says Isaiah, *It wouldn't be enough. You could take all the animals in this bounteous country and sacrifice them and it wouldn't be enough.*

It's not that God has a monstrously overinflated ego. An image like the one above might tempt us to imagine him as being like opera star Jenny Lind in the film *The Greatest Showman*, whose insatiable desire for fame and adulation finds a voice as she sings, "All the glare of a thousand spotlights ... will never be enough". It is a simple matter of fact that if you sacrificed the entire universe to God, you would not exhaust the praise and glory that his holiness deserves. Jenny Lind's character has a deep need to be adored that cannot be fulfilled. God, by contrast, has no needs at all.

Our praise, our service, our devotion, our money—these are things which are good for us to offer God, but he doesn't *need* them. He's not short of money; he's not lacking in self-esteem. God made the universe by speaking—he does not then, in any sense, *need* our help. God is not short-staffed. He is entirely self-sufficient.

Whatever relationship we have with him, then, comes to us not because he needs us, but, amazingly, because he loves us. He blesses us, not because of what we do or can give, but because he wants to bless us.

Just let that sink in. God doesn't need you, but he loves you—and the more you get a sense of the extent of his power and glory and holiness, the more you realise that this is the only possible way that you could relate to him. God is so great that he would be entirely unknowable to us if he didn't actively make himself known. Wonderfully, he has done just this in a variety of ways. One of these ways is in revealing his name.

Names that make sense in one culture don't always make sense in another. My sister taught in Africa for a bit and one of the kids she taught was called Innocent Badger. That sounded funny to us back home as we received my sister's frequently hilarious emails describing her adventures. But we miss out if we allow the significance of names in the Bible to get similarly "lost in translation". They are incredibly meaningful, such that God often changes people's names as a way of shaping their identity. Abram becomes Abraham (the father of many nations). Simon the fisherman becomes Peter (rock), on whom Jesus will build his church. God names lots of people in the Bible, but no one gets to name him. Instead, God reveals his own name: "I AM WHO I AM", or just "I AM" (Yahweh) to his friends (Exodus 3:14).

What does this mean? It means that he is completely and perfectly independent. He exists for one reason and one reason only: because of who he is. No one and nothing else in existence can say that. I exist partly because of my parents, who exist partly because of their parents, and so on. I am not independent; I would not exist unless thousands and thousands of other people before me had met and had children. God though—well, God just "Is".

Theologians who like to use Latin words describe this as God's *aseity*, which basically means God's "being from himself-ness" (I guess we can see why they prefer the Latin). Whatever language we use though, this is the most basic lesson without which we cannot understand God at all. He is self-existent. He is the uncreated Creator of all things. The creation would not exist without him, but he would exist without the creation. I don't know about you, but I can find it hard to imagine the world without me. The evidence suggests, however, that it did a pretty good job of existing without me for most of its history. God, on the other hand, *has* to exist—that is part of the definition of who he is.

Quite a lot follows on from that, as we'll see. But bear in mind the ultimate aim: to see the invisible God a bit more clearly. When we do, it might change more than our sleeping patterns. The twelve things God can't do all express aspects of his nature and character which we can embrace with relief, celebrate with joy, worship with awe—and which, I trust, will help us sleep a little better.

INTERLUDE 1: THE GOD WHO SLEPT

Before we get into the twelve things God can't do, there's one more thing to say by way of introduction. Throughout this book, you'll find a number of interludes like this one, which wrestle with how, in the incarnation, God did the very things he cannot do.

Let's take the example with which we started: God does not sleep. It's an experience entirely alien to God's nature. But that makes one of the stories of Jesus that Matthew, Mark and Luke recount really quite puzzling.

The outline of the story might well be familiar to you. Jesus and his disciples are caught in a terrifying storm of the sort that sometimes sweeps down suddenly on Galilee. His companions, many of them skilled and experienced sailors, desperately demand of Jesus, the comparative landlubber, "Teacher, don't you care if we drown?" In response Jesus gets up and commands the wind and the waves to be silent and the storm is stilled.

There is a pattern, not obvious in English translation, to how Mark tells the story, which makes the calm match the storm (Mark 4:35-41). He depicts the windstorm as "mega" and the calm that follows also as "mega". But there is a third "mega", which describes the disciples' response to Jesus' actions.

They fear a "mega" fear, asking, "Who is this? Even the wind and the waves obey him!" (Mark 4:41). There is only one answer to their question, and that is why they were so afraid. In the Hebrew Scriptures only God commands the elements like that. The disciples end the story more afraid of having Jesus in the boat than they were at having an increasing quantity of the sea in there, because they believed themselves to be in the presence of the living God.

That's not actually the puzzling bit of the story though. The head scratcher is that the disciples have to *wake Jesus up* to ask for his help, because "Jesus was in the stern, sleeping on a cushion" (Mark 4:38).

In this single event, we see Jesus from two perspectives. On the one hand as a weary man, experiencing limitations like our own. On the other hand, he has the power and prerogatives of God himself. How can this be so? It comes down to what we see running right the way through the New Testament: Jesus is both God and man.

This collision of divinity and humanity in one person became the primary source of confusion and division in the early church. Although the New Testament makes it clear that Jesus is fully divine and is to be worshipped along with the Father and the Holy Spirit, some intellectually rigorous people had a problem with accepting this. As we're about to see, some of the things that we know about God don't really fit with what we know about Jesus. In light of this, a very impressive leader in the church, named Arius, refused to accept that Jesus could really be divine at all, but insisted that the Son was just the first and highest of all creatures.

His arguments, which divided the church for a generation, are an example of a danger that Christians have always faced: that of latching onto one biblical idea to the exclusion of all else. Starting with that one idea, they reach a set of conclusions that seem logical, but which contradict something else that Scripture says. Hilary, Bishop of Poitiers, a lifelong opponent of the Arian teaching (he was known as "the hammer of the Arians"), pinned down the basic problem with the Arian approach in his book *De Trinitate*:

All unbelief [in the Son as divine] is foolishness, for it takes such wisdom as its own finite perception can attain, and, measuring infinity by that petty scale, **concludes that what it cannot understand must be impossible.** *Unbelief is the result of incapacity engaged in argument. Men are sure that an event never happened, because they have made up their minds that it could not happen.*[3]

That's fighting talk! But Hilary used strong words because the idea that Jesus is both God and man really matters. Indeed, our salva-tion depends on it. We'll see why that is the case in a later chapter, but for now we note the point: Jesus is both one with us, able to share our limitations, whilst simultaneously be-ing the God who cannot. In this mystery is hidden the depths of the gospel.

To grapple with the enor-mity of the gospel that saves us, we need to come to terms with the things that God cannot do. Only then will we really be able to contemplate just what God *has* done in procuring our salvation. To that end, interspersed between some of the chapters, will be short interludes examining how, in Jesus, God "over-came" these "inabilities" (if I can put it like that) in

---

3 Hilary of Poitiers, "On the Trinity," in *A Select Library of the Nicene and Post-Nicene Fathers of the Christian Church*, Vol. 9a, ed. Philip Schaff and Henry Wace, trans. E. W. Watson et al., Second Series (Christian Literature Company, 1899), p 69. Emphasis mine.

order to save us. We shall discover together that we sleep best at night when we know the God who cannot sleep, but did sleep for us.

1. GOD CAN'T LEARN

"**M**y God is so big, so strong and so mighty there's nothing that he cannot do."

It's too easy to ruin this beloved children's song. One friend of mine is in the habit of singing, "My dog is so big, so strong and so mighty there's nothing that he cannot do (woof woof)". That friend has a lot to answer for (and a disappointingly small dog)—once you've heard his version it's hard not to sing it by mistake.

If no one has ever ruined that song for you before, then, I'm sorry—but it gets worse. We might be used to singing that there's *nothing* that God cannot do and shouting, "That's true". Except, well... it's not exactly true. And it's good that it's not true—because the God who *can't* do things is much greater than the God who is genuinely capable of anything.

This might come as a surprise, because being able to do anything seems like part of the most basic definition of who God is. After all, one of the theological terms we use to describe God is "omnipotent". That word is basically two Latin words stuck together: the word for power, strength or ability (*potentia*) and the word for "all" (*omnis*). So "omnipotent" means having all power, which can easily be expressed as "being able to do anything".

That's a perfectly good explanation, but it's not very precise. The limits of this explanation are highlighted by a hypothetical question that sceptics sometimes ask: "Can God make a rock that's too heavy for him to lift?" If you answer "no" then there's something God can't do—so he's not omnipotent. On the other hand, if you answer "yes" then God's not omnipotent either, because there is at least the possibility of something he can't do. "So," says the sceptic, "your omnipotent God cannot exist". Which is true, if by omnipotent you mean "God can do anything" with absolutely no exceptions. But it doesn't mean that.

After all, the Bible itself contains the phrase "God cannot". In 2 Timothy 2:13 we read that God "cannot disown himself". We'll save the significance of that one for the very end of the book, but for now it simply proves that there is at least one thing that God can't do. So all that effort in coming up with a question about a rock in the hope that God won't be able to lift it turns out to be a waste of time. Neither the Bible nor the Christian tradition has ever really claimed that "there's nothing that he cannot do" in that absolute sense.

"Sure," you might be thinking to yourself, "but that's cheating. Those things don't count." After all, denying God is the mark of a fool in Scripture (Psalm 14:1), and who wants a foolish God? To say that God cannot deny his own existence—or that he cannot lie, or that he cannot be tempted by evil—is a *good* thing. In the words of Anselm, the tenth-century Archbishop of Canterbury:

> *He who is capable of these things is capable of what is not for his good, and of what he ought not to do; and the more capable of them he is, the more power have adversity and perversity against him; and the less has he himself against these.*

Which is really a way of saying that some sorts of ability are really just weaknesses. To be unable to do wrong is a strength even if it is expressed as an inability.

But there are also things God can't do that we tend to think of as good things to be able to do. Take, for example, the theme of this chapter: God cannot learn. How is that a good thing? After all, if "Nick cannot learn" had been written on my school report, I wouldn't have been keen to take it home to my parents. But thinking about why it is that God cannot learn can actually help us to see his glory more clearly.

Try thinking of it like this: imagine a water barrel, like you might find in a garden or allotment. If we were told that this barrel cannot hold any more water than it currently does, we could imagine lots of possible reasons for that. It might already be completely full, so that it is physically impossible to add any further liquid: there is simply no space. It might be split, such that any new water will just spill out. Or there might be a blockage in the only opening to the container and that stops any more water getting in.

If you think about the brain as being like that barrel, and information as water, we can think of similar reasons why someone might not be able to learn. When I was at school, sometimes my brain just felt crammed full and it couldn't accept any more information. It was at capacity. Once I banged my head so hard in the playground that for a while I didn't even know what day it was—information kept leaking away. Much of the time I was so busy thinking about sport that I wasn't paying attention and the information couldn't get in, like with the blocked drainpipe. In each of those cases, my inability to learn came from my limitations. But when we say that God can't learn, it's not for any of those reasons.

Let's stay with the idea of a water barrel. Try to imagine one much too big to fit in your garden. In fact, imagine that this barrel already contains all the water in the world—more than that, it contains all the water in the universe. In this case, it is impossible for that barrel to get any fuller—not because of any limitation in its capacity to hold water, but because there simply isn't any more water to add. That is what we mean when we say that God cannot learn. It's not because of a lack of power on his part but because there is no conceivable kind of knowledge or piece of data that he does not already possess.

In Psalm 139, David presents us with a breathtaking account of God's intimate knowledge of him. Before you read on, I would encourage you to read Psalm 139 slowly, with three questions in mind: What does God know? How does he know this? What effect does that have on David?

With that done, let's walk through the psalm together:

> *¹ You have searched me, LORD,*
> *   and you know me.*
> *² You know when I sit and when I rise;*
> *   you perceive my thoughts from afar.*
> *³ You discern my going out and my lying down;*
> *   you are familiar with all my ways. (v 1-3)*

The theme of the psalm is stated in verse one: "You have searched me, LORD, and you know me". The focus is God's knowledge—specifically his knowledge of the writer, King David.

It all starts fairly innocuously, with the kind of knowledge that any moderately competent private detective could expect to have of their mark: "You know when I sit and when I rise".

The next phrase sounds a little more intrusive: "You perceive my thoughts from afar". Even so, this isn't totally beyond normal human experience. Most of us can tell something of someone else's emotional state by observing their facial expressions and body language, particularly when we know them well. So "you perceive my thoughts from afar" speaks perhaps of a high degree of understanding of someone, and even a deep intimate knowledge.

Verse 3 takes us back into the domain of the private investigator: "You discern my going out and my lying down; you are familiar with all my ways". Still, it's pretty impressive to have this sort of knowledge of all eight billion human beings on the planet. That's an unimaginable amount of data (although not beyond the realms of Google's ambitions). But even then, we're still thinking in terms of the sort of knowledge that we possess, just on a gigantic scale. What's coming next puts God's knowledge in a different category altogether...

> *⁴ Before a word is on my tongue*
> *you, LORD, know it completely.*
> *⁵ You hem me in behind and before,*
> *and you lay your hand upon me.*
> *⁶ Such knowledge is too wonderful for me,*
> *too lofty for me to attain. (v 4-6)*

Suddenly we are transported to another dimension, an entirely different mode of knowledge. God, according to verse 4, not only knows what *is* but what *will be*. David picks up the theme again in verses 15-16:

> *¹⁵ My frame was not hidden from you*
> *when I was made in the secret place,*
> *when I was woven together in the depths of the*
> *earth.*
> *¹⁶ Your eyes saw my unformed body;*

*all the days ordained for me were written in your
   book
before one of them came to be. (v 15-16)*

Even before there was a David to know, God knew him. More extraordinary than that even, God knew *everything*— David's whole life was an open book to God even before he drew breath (v 15).

Just think about that for a moment. God knows the whole you, perfectly, from beginning to end, for the whole of your life. He's not getting to know you. He's not making memories, or building up a file on you. He knows it all already—even your future—in every detail.

Our minds naturally rebel against this sort of picture of God. We struggle to fit it with our perception of the nature of time. We raise questions about our freedom, imagining that if this were true it would remove all sense of responsibility for our actions. We will come back to some of these things in future chapters (pun intended I suppose), but for now that is not our focus. We have asked the psalmist, "What does God know?" and the answer has come back as "everything". But in the process, the psalmist has redefined "everything" to include things that we don't really consider knowable.

That doesn't just mean the future; God also sees the heart. When David says that the Lord knows David's words "completely" (v 4), I take it to mean that God understands every possible nuance of David's communication. Beyond the meaning of the words themselves or the tone of voice in which they're said, God perceives the *roots* of the words in David's heart and mind before the thought even comes into his head.

As we think about this, our second question comes into play: "How does God know this?" How can anyone have access to this kind of knowledge? It's so beyond our experience that it seems kind of... unlikely.

This might be because we tend to think of God as a bigger version of ourselves, sitting up in heaven receiving and managing information in much the same ways that we do. Some of our knowledge comes to us intuitively, but most of what we know—what day it is, what cows smell like, where the supermarket is—comes through experience. So, we imagine that God knows things in much the same way. We picture him receiving sense data—sounds, smells, sights and so on—and then processing that information.

Granted, we acknowledge that God must have some supernatural "senses" in addition to our own. Anyone who has ever prayed silently presumably believes that God can read their thoughts. They are right, he can—but not in exactly the way that we imagine. We think of God "hearing" the voice in our heads and so we think of the content of our thoughts as something that God receives via some means or other.

But this doesn't account for how God is able to know David's words before they are on his tongue (v 4). David's future self is known to God in ways that are unknown, and unknowable, to David. This goes beyond "hearing" or predicting David's inner monologue. Which brings us back to the question: How does God know this?!

We get the answer in verse 13. In the previous verses, David explores the possibilities for concealment offered by the height, depth and breadth of geography ("If I go up to the heavens ... if I make my bed in the depths ... if I settle on the far side of the sea", v 8-9) and the removal of sense data ("If I say, 'Surely the darkness will hide me'", v 11). None of these can prevent God's knowledge, however, as he is there wherever David goes (v 8) and "even the darkness will not be dark" to him (v 12). At the end of this futile search for cover David finally answers our question, signalling it with the word "For". Here's the reason God knows all he knows in the way that he knows it, independently of sense data:

> ¹³ For you created my inmost being;
>   you knit me together in my mother's womb.
> ¹⁴ I praise you because I am fearfully and
>   wonderfully made;
>   your works are wonderful,
>   I know that full well.
> ¹⁵ My frame was not hidden from you
>   when I was made in the secret place,
>   when I was woven together in the depths of the
>   earth.
> ¹⁶ Your eyes saw my unformed body;

> *all the days ordained for me were*
>   *written in your book*
> *before one of them came to be. (v 13-16)*

How can God know? He knows by creation. Which is to say that he knows things in exactly the opposite way than we do. The great African theologian Augustine expressed this brilliantly in *The City of God*:

> *The world could not have been known to us unless it existed. It could not have existed unless it had been known to God.*[4]

This, ultimately, is why God cannot learn. He knows all of reality by making it, and so there is no information that he does not already have. This includes every motion of every molecule, every atom, every subatomic particle, throughout the universe from its beginning to its end, and all the interactions and effects between all those moving pieces. He knows them perfectly and instantly and does not rely on their existence for him to know them. God is not like you. He is unimaginably great.

All this means that we will never understand God entirely from God's point of view. We are dealing with a God who is beyond our comprehension. As creatures made in God's image, our minds are uniquely fitted to know and

---

4 Augustine of Hippo, "The City of God," in *St. Augustine's City of God and Christian Doctrine, A Select Library of the Nicene and Post-Nicene Fathers of the Christian Church*, Vol. 2, ed. Philip Schaff, trans. Marcus Dods, First Series (Christian Literature Company, 1887), p 211.

understand him—yet when even the greatest minds try to grasp his greatness, they reach a point where they have to give up and worship instead.

This is where our answer to that third question is important: What effect does this have on David? In short, David is utterly overwhelmed by God:

> *17 How precious to me are your thoughts, God!*
> *How vast is the sum of them!*
> *18 Were I to count them,*
> *they would outnumber the grains of sand –*
> *when I awake, I am still with you. (v 17-18)*

Try to imagine counting all the grains of sand in just one teaspoon of the stuff. Now imagine how many teaspoons it would take to fill just one sandpit. Then consider how much sand there is on just one beach. Then repeat for just one desert. When, like David, we contemplate the overwhelming majesty of God's mind, we have no option but to worship.

True worship is to treat something or someone as the very highest good—and, on the flip side, to consider whatever opposes that good as evil and threatening. We all know what it feels like to get defensive over someone we love when we see them being targeted by someone else. That's something like what is going on in verses 19-22:

> *19 If only you, God, would slay the wicked!*
> *Away from me, you who are bloodthirsty!*
> *20 They speak of you with evil intent;*

your adversaries misuse your name.
[21] *Do I not hate those who hate you, LORD,*
and abhor those who are in rebellion against you?
[22] *I have nothing but hatred for them;*
I count them my enemies. (v 19-20)

David is so in awe of God that he sees all reality as revolving around him. From this standpoint, David can't help but align himself with God's view of sin. He sees it as an assault on all that is good; he sees it for the empty, dark embrace of evil that it is. And he is repulsed. In that moment, he sees God's righteous judgment as the only thing that can bring release.

For some of us, these verses look too much like the ugly self-righteous judgmentalism that has characterised the church in its most unattractive moments. For David, though, his call for judgment on the wicked results in self-reflection. In seeing sin for what it is, he sees his own sin for what it is and yearns for cleansing:

[23] *Search me, God, and know my heart;*
test me and know my anxious thoughts.
[24] *See if there is any offensive way in me,*
and lead me in the way everlasting. (v 23-24)

In Psalm 139 David models a pattern that should be evident in the life of every believer: that of looking to God's goodness, recognising the horror of sin in our own hearts, and admitting our need for divine remedy. Viewed from this side of the cross, it becomes even more pointed. The broken body of the Son of God speaks more eloquently than any other image of God's horror at sin. It reminds us that the judgment that David calls for would rightly have fallen on us, save for the intervention of Jesus who bore it in himself. The judgmental Christian knows neither himself nor the gospel very well.

Consider the flip side of this for a moment. The God who cannot learn already knows the depths of your heart. There is literally nothing that has ever been hidden from him, and nothing *could* ever be hidden from him. So the deepest recesses of your heart, the dark places which you try to conceal and hide from yourself and others, are an open book to the God who made you. In her brilliant book *Confronting Christianity*, Rebecca McLaughlin observes that "all our [human] relationships hinge, to some extent, on hiding".[5] Amazingly, there is one relationship where this is not so. The "you" Jesus died for is not the sanitized "Sunday best" version of you: Jesus died for "you", warts and all. There is nothing new that he could learn about you that would put him off. God really knows you and, knowing you, he really loves you. What a glorious freedom to know that you are known completely, and still loved. What a relief!

And that leads us to another answer to the question, "What effect does God's knowledge have on David?" that we skipped over. In verse 18, reflecting on the immensity

---

5 Rebecca McLaughlin, *Confronting Christianity: 12 Hard Questions for the World's Largest Religion* (Crossway, 2019), p 213.

of God's knowledge of him, David says, "When I awake, I am still with you".

How does David react to knowing God in this way?

You've got it. He sleeps.

2. GOD CAN'T BE SURPRISED

"Psychic Fair cancelled due to unforeseen circumstances." It's an old joke, but it's one that illustrates our ambivalence about claims to see into the future. On the one hand, many of us are fascinated by the prospect of a glimpse of what is to come. We instinctively believe that there is a future to be seen—and jump at the chance to see it. We devour boxsets set in eerily realistic dystopian futures; we cast our eye down the horoscopes because "you never know". On the other hand, many of us are deeply sceptical about anyone or anything who claims to be able to see the future. After all, the future doesn't exist yet, so how can it be known?

But God *does* know the future. As we saw in the previous chapter, God doesn't need things to exist in order to know them. In fact, God needs to know them in order for them to exist. When we say that "God can't be surprised", what we are really saying is that God knows the future as perfectly as he knows the past or the present.

This can serve as a great comfort. When we make promises, they are always contingent. In the spring of 2020 my calendar was full of commitments. I had agreed in good faith to be at such and such a place to meet with such and such a person at such and such a time. I had even promised to marry some people (to one another, I hasten to add). But due to an unforeseen change in circumstances (namely, a global pandemic), I no longer had the ability to do the things that had seemed entirely within my power when I scheduled them. In contrast, though, the God who knows the future will not be thwarted by surprising turns of events. Every promise he makes, he makes in full knowledge that he can keep it. He cannot be surprised, so he will never let you down.

So far, so good. But there is a scary set of implications lurking in the shadows around that reassuring claim about God's knowledge of the future. If God knows the future in that sort of way, then does that mean the future is completely fixed? In which case, you and I are not free. I may think that I have chosen to use an hour or so before the kids got up this morning to write this, and you might think that you have chosen to read it—but in reality, we are both blindly following a script that was written before the dawn of time. We have no freedom, no agency, no choice. We are effectively passengers on a fairground ride—the kind with a fake steering wheel in front of you. You can pretend to be in control if you would like to, but you are not.

That seems like a pretty bleak way of looking at life. After all, one of the things that we think of as giving human life dignity is a sense of agency; that is, the ability to act independently and make decisions. It also seems to be an important thing in the Bible, because agency is a prerequisite for moral responsibility. We don't sentence an axe to jail for murder, we sentence the person who wielded it. The axe had no agency, so it has no culpability. According to the Bible, human beings *are* guilty when they do things wrong. They *do* have agency and so are culpable (Romans 1:18-23).

So how do we hold that together with the idea that God knows the future perfectly? Some theologians square the circle by saying that God doesn't, in fact, know the future. Amongst them is Greg Boyd, who argues that God has perfect knowledge of what can be known, but that the future doesn't exist and therefore can't be known:

If we have been given freedom, we create the reality of our decisions by making them. And until we make them, they don't exist. Thus, in my view at least, there simply isn't anything to know until we make it there to know. So, God can't foreknow the good or bad decisions of the people He creates until He creates these people and they, in turn, create their decisions.[6]

---

6 Greg Boyd, *Letters From a Skeptic* (David C Cook, 2008), p 39.

That seems like a neat solution to the problem, but can it really be that simple?

Take, for instance, the story of Joseph (Genesis 37 – 50). He is sold into slavery by his jealous brothers, but by an extraordinary route effectively becomes the prime minister of Egypt, the dominant world power of the day. As Prime Minister he presides over a grain-storage programme that allows Egypt to weather a famine of unprecedented severity. As such, he also becomes the saviour of his brothers, who come to Egypt seeking food. At the end of the story, when their father Jacob dies, the brothers are terrified that Joseph will seek revenge. Instead, Joseph says:

> *Don't be afraid. Am I in the place of God? You*
> *intended to harm me, but God intended it for good*
> *to accomplish what is now being done, the saving of*
> *many lives. (50:19-20)*

Who does Joseph see as responsible for what happened? Well, in truth, it's complicated. On the one hand, you would have to say it was God. He stood behind the actions of Joseph's wicked and envious brothers, who only sold him into slavery because that was more profitable than straightforward murder (37:26-7). But on the other hand, his brothers did what they wanted to do ("You intended to harm me"). Did God not only know what the brothers would do, but in some way plan it and make it happen? Joseph believed so. But that didn't mean that the brothers were not free or responsible for their actions.

These two ideas—that the brothers followed their own plan, and that they followed God's plan—seem incompatible to us. We can't see how both those things can be true. At this point, we might find ourselves drawn to the arguments that Greg Boyd and others make. Their position, known as Open Theism, makes its own kind of sense, but we do need to understand the exchange that is being made.

Think back to Hilary of Poitiers' critique of those who *"conclude that what it cannot understand must be impossible"*. Ultimately, the choice is between accepting the biblical account and what you instinctively believe must be true. It's a choice we all face when we come to things about God which we can't understand—and once you start looking there are plenty of those! We must all decide where we believe ultimate authority to speak about God to be based. Hilary's answer to that dilemma in his book *De Trinitate*, is the answer that underpins this book and all true Christian theology:

> *Since then we are to discourse of the things of God, let us assume that God has full knowledge of Himself, and bow with humble reverence to His words. For He Whom we can only know through His own utterances is the fitting witness concerning Himself.*[7]

---

7 Hilary of Poitiers, "On the Trinity," in *A Select Library of the Nicene and Post-Nicene Fathers of the Christian Church*, Vol. 9a, ed. Philip Schaff and Henry Wace, trans. E. W. Watson et al., Second Series (Christian Literature Company, 1899), p 45.

So then, we need to be clear about what God has said in Scripture concerning himself, the future and us. The claim of the Bible is that God cannot be surprised. He really does know everything that lies in the future of his universe. In Isaiah 44, for example, we read the following:

> *Who then is like me? Let him proclaim it.*
> *Let him declare and lay out before me*
> *what has happened since I established*
> *my ancient people,*
> *and what is yet to come—*
> *yes, let them foretell what will come. (Isaiah 44:7)*

God, as Creator, is distinguished from the idols of the nations by his knowledge of the future. In this verse it's as though God invites the idols of the surrounding nations—idols to which the people of Israel constantly felt themselves drawn—to a "god factor" contest. It's a winner-takes-all scenario, and God sets the test: a history exam, where half the questions are about the future. No pretender to deity could pass that paper: the God of Abraham, Isaac and Jacob gets 100%.

It's true that there are a small number of texts in the Bible that can appear to suggest that God didn't see something coming, such as 1 Samuel 15:35: "The LORD regretted that he had made Saul king over Israel". But a far greater number presuppose that God knows the future exhaustively. Steve Roy, a theologian from Trinity Evangelical Divinity School, has identified over 4,500 texts that speak of God's intimate knowledge or control of the future. By contrast he identified only 105 texts, like 1 Samuel 15:35 above, that appear to suggest that God doesn't know the future or receives new information.

Of course, if those 105 texts actually *do* deny that God knows the future, then we have the problem that Scripture contradicts itself. We'll come back to the 1 Samuel passage in another chapter, and I trust that your mind will be set at rest on this. For now, suffice it to say that neither this nor any other passage actually suggests that God doesn't know the future from our perspective. He really cannot be surprised.

Although, having said that, I think there *is* a good reason to say that God doesn't know the future.

"Now hold on a minute!" I hear you say, "didn't you literally *just* say that God knows the future perfectly?" Why, yes, I did (thanks for noticing). But it's all about perspective. Our problem with all this comes down to the nature of time.

In one sense, as Greg Boyd argues, it is logically impossible to know the future—the future doesn't exist, so it is not there to be known. It's a bit like the old saying that "tomorrow never comes". Today used to be tomorrow, but the today in which I write this is yesterday to you, who are reading this in what is "tomorrow" from my perspective now, but very much "today" from yours. No wonder that Augustine, one of the cleverest people ever to set pen to paper, wrote, "What, then, is time? If no one asks me, I know; if I want to explain it to a questioner, I do not know."[8] When we actually try to think about what time is, we quickly realise that it is a bit like asking a fish about water—and the sorts of faces we tend to pull in response are quite similar to what you get from a fish too (mouth open, eyes uncomprehending).

When it comes to talking about God and time, it gets even harder. The reason for this, is that God exists without time—outside of it and independent from it. Think about the very first words of the Bible: "In the beginning God created the heavens and the earth" (Genesis 1:1). The creation of reality seems to mark the "beginning"—that is, the start gun on reality, the beginning of time itself. Professor Stephen Hawking in his *Brief History of Time* put it like this: "The concept of time has no meaning before the beginning of the universe".[9] Augustine made this point too: "What time could there be that you had not created? ... You made it, for time could not pass before You made time".[10] Time and space go together: they are aspects of the created order. God exists independently of these things: he is timeless.

As timeless, God does not know things one after the other, but knows them all at once. (Although notice that I can't

---

8 Augustine, *Confessions*, ed. Michael P. Foley (Hackett Publishing Company, 2006), p 242.

9 Stephen Hawking, *A Brief History of Time: From the Big Bang to Black Holes* (Bantam, 1995), p 9.

10 Augustine, *Confessions*, ed. Michael P. Foley (Hackett Publishing Company, 2006), p 241-242.

find a way of expressing that without suggesting time!) The past, the present and the future (from our perspective) are all perfectly present to God. The history of the world does not unfold before his eyes—he knows it all in one perfect act of cognition. In that sense, God doesn't know "the future", he just knows everything that it is possible to know, including the position and movement of every subatomic particle (and their effect on each other), from the beginning to the end of time.

To say that God cannot be surprised is simply to turn up the volume on the idea that God cannot learn. Not only does he know everything that it is possible to know, he knows everything that it is impossible for creatures to know too.

This does make thinking about God difficult. We cannot imagine what timelessness looks like or means. Even the language we use is so "time-infected" that we find that we don't quite have the words to use to talk about God's being. Words such as "timeless" or "eternal" are helpful, but they are just negations—expressing what his being is not like.

All of which brings us back to the fact that God is not like us. The greatest of human minds are just too puny to grasp the entirety of who God is. His relationship to time is so unimaginably different from anything we have ever experienced or imagined, that we are left having to accept that we will never fully understand him. Indeed, our God can only be truly known once we accept that we cannot know him by ourselves. As Hilary put it, God is someone who "we can only know through his own utterances".

Knowing the God who cannot be surprised is, however, the secret to living at peace in an uncertain world. The mood music in the West is pretty downbeat at the moment. In fact, it has been for some time. Woody Allen, although a controversial figure to say the least, has always had a knack of expressing the angst of living in the modern world. In his 1980 book of essays, *Side Effects*, he wrote, "More than at any other time in history, mankind faces a crossroads. One path leads to despair and utter hopelessness. The other to total extinction. Let us pray we have the wisdom to choose correctly." More than 40 years on, that statement seems to capture our present situation even better than the last days of the Cold War that it initially described.

The looming threats have changed in the last four decades, but the mood remains the same. Climate change is now—particularly amongst the young—described as an emergency, to the extent that one influential movement to grow out of this calls itself "Extinction Rebellion". The anxiety about the future contained therein is palpable. As I write, we are in the midst of a global public health emergency that seems likely to change the face of civilisation for a generation. Those immune to climate anxiety have found, in Covid-19, something to despair over. As the economist John Maynard Keynes put it: *"In the long run* we are all dead".[11] In a world without God, optimism about the future is a sign that you aren't looking far enough ahead.

But if you walk hand in hand with the God who already knows the future, and who makes promises about it, then at the end of each day you can lay down your head in peace. Imagine going to the cinema with a friend. Partway through, the heroine of the film looks certain to die, and your insides are in knots. Your friend leans over and says, "Don't worry—she makes it in the end". If they haven't already seen the film, such an assurance is meaningless. But if they *have* already seen the film, then you are more likely to find their words comforting. (Or annoying, if you hate spoilers.)

When God says, "Never will I leave you; never will I forsake you" (Hebrews 13:5), that's not a prediction. He has seen the film. He knows the end of the story. It isn't merely that he is committed to you in the present and, looking forward, can't see how that might change. He knows that it won't. He knows the whole story of your life, and the whole story of the world, and "never will I leave you" is a statement of fact.

This being so, we can say with the apostle Paul: "I am convinced that neither death nor life, neither angels nor demons, neither the present nor the future, nor any

---

11 John Maynard Keynes, *A Tract on Monetary Reform* (Macmillan and Co., 1929), p 80. Emphasis mine.

powers, neither height nor depth, nor anything else in all creation, will be able to separate us from the love of God that is in Christ Jesus our Lord" (Romans 8:38-9). Not even the future can separate us from the love of the God who has already been there.

3. GOD CAN'T CHANGE
HIS MIND

In October 1980, UK Prime Minister Margaret Thatcher found her government's economic policy was under severe scrutiny. Unemployment was rising, the economy was shrinking, and Thatcher was facing calls to change direction. Her speech at the Conservative party conference addressed this expected "U-turn" with a phrase that would define her career: "You turn if you want to. The lady's not for turning!"

To her supporters, this was evidence of her resolution, her exceptional ability to lead and ultimately of her strength. We want our leaders to lead, and she was certainly doing that. To her opponents, though, it was a sign of destructive inflexibility. Mrs Thatcher's refusal to change course proved her to be wedded to an ideology that did not work, unable to change her mind in the face of the evidence. As one saying goes, "When the facts change, I change my mind..." Never changing one's mind, in a world of flux, is less a virtue than a pathology.

Whichever side of the fence one might stand about a particular politician, it's pretty easy to see how the ability to change one's mind can be a double-edged sword, and not just in politics. Wherever someone is called on to lead, if you never change, you are stubborn, and probably stupid; if you do it too easily, then you are irresolute and given to flip-flop.

Surely what we want from our leaders is iron resolve, coupled with an appropriate humility in the face of reality. Our ideal leader would be willing to change their mind if the facts demanded it, but would only ever do so *if* the facts demanded it.

Even better than that would be a leader who began with perfect information, and perfect intuitions about what to do in the face of that information, and thus never needed to make a "U-turn". But we know that no mortal person could ever offer such leadership. As human beings we are constantly vulnerable to what the statistician and author Nassim Nicholas Taleb calls "Black Swan events". If you haven't come across the concept before, it's pretty simple. During the Middle Ages and into the early modern era, Western Europeans believed that all swans must be white. So much so that "like a black swan" was an expression used to describe something that was impossible. No one could have predicted what the Dutch navigator Willem de

Vlamingh would find on his arrival in Western Australia in 1697. On the river which runs through what is now Perth, he became the first European to witness that most unimaginable of creatures: the black swan. Taleb took this event as the theme of his influential book, *The Black Swan*, which highlights the limits of human knowledge for making predictions and policy. The most significant events that shape our lives and economies are "Black Swans"—entirely unpredictable.

So, no human leader could possibly make decisions with sufficient information to never need to change their mind. The available information is always changing, and it is predictably unpredictable.

But God is not like us. He does not change his mind. In fact, he does not change his mind *because* he is not like us. Statements in the Bible about God not changing his mind frequently put those two things together. For instance: "He who is the Glory of Israel does not lie or change his mind; for he is not a human being, that he should change his mind" (1 Samuel 15:29).

It's not just that God doesn't change his mind—it's that he can't. Think about it like this. Why does anyone change their mind? The impulse must either be internal or external. Either something changes inside me—perhaps as a result of something as simple as a good (or a bad) night's sleep; or, circumstances change—for example, I changed my mind this morning about what to wear, because when I got downstairs I realised it was going to be a much colder day than yesterday's weather forecast suggested.

In God's case, there are neither internal nor external reasons for change. If he really is the great I AM—the one who "is who he is" eternally—then change from the inside is impossible. For a perfect being, all change is change for the worse. Change driven from the outside is likewise impossible, since it presupposes that new information is received. As we've already seen, God can't learn or be surprised. He never receives "new" information, so he never has any external reason to change his mind.

At this point, you might point to moments in Scripture where God does actually seem to change his mind. One such incident is in Exodus 32. After God has rescued his people from slavery in Egypt and brought them through the Red Sea, they arrive at Mount Sinai. Moses goes up the mountain to meet with God. But whilst Moses is up the mountain, learning from God how his people could live with him, the people are busy constructing a god out of gold, in the shape of a calf, to worship.

Because of this, God tells Moses that he wants to "destroy" Israel after their rebellion and start again from scratch with Moses. Moses intercedes though, pleading with God on behalf of the people. In the end, we're told that God "relented and did not bring on his people the disaster he had threatened" (Exodus 32:14). In other words, God changed his mind.

However, when you look at the words of Moses' prayer, the whole episode looks a bit different: "Remember your servants Abraham, Isaac and Israel, to whom you swore by your own self: 'I will make your descendants as numerous as the stars in the sky and I will give your descendants all this land I promised them, and it will be their inheritance for ever'" (Exodus 32:13). Instead of asking God to change his mind, Moses actually requests that he does not do so.

Similarly, we mentioned 1 Samuel 15:35 in the previous chapter: "And the LORD regretted that he had made Saul king over Israel". Again, this looks like a clear example of God changing his mind. Again, though, the immediate context makes us question that appearance. Just six verses before, Samuel speaks prophetically to Saul with these words: "He who is the Glory of Israel does not lie or change his mind; for he is not a human being, that he should change his mind" (1 Samuel 15:29). So either the writer of 1 Samuel was inconsistent and rather incompetent in putting together his account, or the phrase "the LORD regretted" is supposed to tell us more about God's attitude to Saul's failures as king than to his own previous decisions.

So, that's the big take-home message from this chapter: God can't change his mind. But why does it matter?

Please don't imagine that this is all a bit too abstract to be of "use" to you as an ordinary believer. First of all, we can sometimes be far too quick to associate value with "usefulness". If we can't see how something is going to fix a problem for us, or give us a skill we don't possess, or enhance a quality that we'd love to see in ourselves, then many of us conclude that it's not really worth our time. But not so fast.

Traffic lights are useful—they help prevent accidents and keep the traffic flowing in all the directions it needs to. It's much harder to say that Michelangelo's sculpture David is useful—it has no flat surface that you can put things on and it doesn't produce anything. Yet we instinctively know that the sculptural masterpiece has more value to humanity than a set of traffic lights. Last month a careless driver demolished the traffic lights outside my house (it wasn't me!). It didn't make the news. But in 1991, when Piero Cannata used a hammer he had concealed under his coat to attack the statue, damaging the toes on the left foot, it was reported around the world. There is an intrinsic value to beauty and goodness that goes far beyond obvious categories of utility. After all, in the Garden of Eden we're told that the trees provided pleasure for the eyes as well as food. The kingdom of God is not utilitarian.

Here's where I'm going with this. At the heart of the Christian life is worship—praise, adoration and devotion given to God. We worship God for who he is. Therefore, if something is true about him, it is worth knowing it. Any true thing I know about God enriches me enormously, even if I'm not sure at first what difference it makes to my life. If it fuels my wonder at who God is—if it reminds me just how much greater he is than anything in creation—it has surpassing value.

As long as I think of God as "like me, just bigger" I am a stranger to real worship. As long as I think he is comparable with myself, my worship will be that of a fan, not a creature. God's knowledge—the scope, the mode and the extent of it—is such that I cannot even begin to grasp what it looks like for God to know things, let alone aspire to having knowledge like his. The God who made me is beyond my imagination, but he knows me, he cares for me, and is interested enough in a relationship with me that he has found a way to make himself known to a mind as puny as mine. I will spend all eternity getting to know him better and never get to the end of him. I will spend endless days learning new and deeper reasons to praise him. If my praise now is without wonder then it has little in common with the praise of heaven.

Mind you, none of this is to say that we are dealing with abstract ideas about God that have no impact on life. In Scripture, the fact that God doesn't change his mind is something that underpins the certainty of his promises. Take, for instance, the story of Balaam, who was employed by the Moabite king Balak to curse Israel as they camped on the outskirts of the promised land (Numbers 22 – 24). No matter how hard Balak tried to get Balaam to pronounce a curse on God's people, all that Balaam could do was bless them. On the second attempt to call down cursing,

God spoke a message through the renegade prophet as follows: "God is not human that he should lie, not a human being, that he should change his mind. Does he speak and then not act? Does he promise and not fulfil?" (Numbers 23:19).

Those rhetorical questions highlight the believer's rock-solid grounds for confidence. If God has spoken, the matter is done. Much frustration in our house comes from my habit of saying (with the best of intentions) that I will do something later, but then running out of time and not being able to follow through on a particular action. Despite fine-sounding words, the shelf remains unaffixed to the wall, the bin in the kitchen continues to overflow, and the washing on the line outside is getting an "extra rinse". Unlike me, God always follows through. If he has promised to bless his people, there is nothing anyone can do to prevent it. It doesn't matter how hard our enemies might try to talk God out of his promises, as in the case of Balaam. His words never fail. His words express his mind, and the Lord is not for turning.

Our God does not and will not and cannot change his mind. He never wakes up in a bad mood. He never forgets an agreement he's made or a conversation he's had. He will never find something better or more convenient to do than keep his promises to you. He will never find someone more interesting or more strategic to invest his efforts in. He is never blind-sided by new information or swayed by popular opinion. He is not looking to back out on what he has started. He is committed in his affection; resolute in his justice; determined in his plans. Nothing and no one can throw him off course.

And so it is that God's inability to change his mind becomes a cause for God's people to sleep securely. We know that he will never reconsider a single promise or go back on even one word he has spoken, so we can build our entire lives on his word and trust him completely.

The letter to the Hebrews was written to Christians who were suffering and tempted to give up on Jesus. The writer's central argument is that only Jesus can offer lasting peace with God, because he has established a new and better covenant that cannot be broken; therefore to give up on Jesus is to give up on God. As part of this argument, the writer repeatedly picks up on the fourth verse of Psalm 110, in which David looked ahead to his superior descendant who would be both priest and king:

> *The Lord has sworn*
> *and will not change his mind:*
> *"You are a priest for ever." (Hebrews 7:21)*

The writer's reason for quoting the verse is to highlight the security of God's promises in Jesus. "Because of this oath" he says, "Jesus has become the guarantor of a better covenant" (v 22). That word "guarantor" is very powerful. It used to be translated as "surety" and it refers to someone who would take all the legal implications of someone else's debt or obligation. The guarantor could be subject to "ruin and imprisonment, and even reduction to slavery, because they were 'subject to the same penalties as those for whom they offered themselves as guarantees.'"[12] Jesus himself, the Son of God, stands as our surety; he absolutely guarantees that God will accept us as his people. His work on our behalf cannot fail unless he fails, as it is based on God's oath, and God "will not change his mind".

There's something immensely comforting about certainty. We all know what it is like to feel edgy until something that has been promised is delivered. "There's many a slip twixt cup and lip," as they used to say. One of the great anxieties I see regularly in the course of my ministry is in people who wonder whether they will really receive what Jesus has promised in the end. I've lost count of the times that I have asked a seriously unwell person—committed Christian people and members of my church—if they are ready to meet God, only to receive a reply along the lines of, "Well, I just have to hope that God will accept me".

It seems too good to be true that we might be *sure* of eternal life. Perhaps it feels arrogant or presumptuous to say that we are certain. Yet the implication of the promise of God is that we *can* be certain. If you put yourself in Jesus' hands, your place in God's kingdom is as certain as his. It is settled; there is no "maybe" or "hopefully" or "probably" about it.

---

12 Ceslas Spicq and James D. Ernest, *Theological Lexicon of the New Testament* (Hendrickson Publishers, 1994), p 392.

The apostle Paul was not afraid to speak of these things with certainty. So much so that in Romans 8:29-30, he can start off talking about Christians as people "God foreknew" and goes on in an unbroken chain of saving acts that ends with him describing Christians as those "[God] also glorified". Glory is something that lies in our future— it's what comes at the return of Christ, when everything he won for his people is finally theirs, and when we will see God "face to face". Yet, amazingly, Paul speaks of it in the past tense—as something that has already happened. Why? Because God does not change his mind. He will finish what he has started. He does not speak and then fail to act. We can rest peacefully, and indeed, rest in peace, because God's promises are utterly secure.

INTERLUDE 2: GOD WENT TO SCHOOL

We know very little about Jesus' childhood. Aside from the events surrounding his birth, the only Gospel that tells us anything about it is Luke. He recounts a story of Jesus, aged twelve, going missing in Jerusalem.

It's a story that resonates with parents everywhere. On a couple of occasions, I have known the dread chill of realising that one of our kids was missing. Once after church, our then three-year-old shut herself in a cupboard in the hall to read quietly whilst parents chatted for too long over coffee. On realising that she was missing we experienced a few minutes of blind panic searching for her. We feared that she might have left the building and I set off sprinting around local streets praying that she would not come to harm. The feeling of powerlessness and desperation that swept over me in those moments still echoes in my heart as I imagine Mary and Joseph combing the crowded streets of Jerusalem for three days looking for their son.

What must the relief have been like when they finally found him? "After three days they found him in the temple courts, sitting among the teachers, listening to them and asking them questions. Everyone who heard him was amazed at his understanding and his answers" (v 46-47). Luke brilliantly draws us into the earthy reality of the situation by matching the wonder of the onlookers with the exasperation of Jesus' parents: "When his parents saw him, they were astonished. His mother said to him, 'Son, why have you treated us like this? Your father and I have been anxiously searching for you'" (v 48).

What feels like the climax of the story comes in Jesus' reply: "Why were you searching for me? ... Didn't you know I had to be in my Father's house?" (v 49). To readers of Luke's Gospel, who have just read about the miraculous events surrounding Jesus' birth, this all makes sense. His parents though, "did not understand what he was saying to them," although "his mother treasured all these things in her heart" (v 50-51).

After two millennia in which millions of people around the world have worshipped this Jesus as God himself, and in which whole civilisations have been rebuilt and reshaped around this worship, the extraordinary religious knowledge and insight displayed by Jesus the tween-ager is in some ways the easiest part of the story to connect with and accept. But it is not where Luke ends the episode. He tells us that Jesus returned to Nazareth with his parents and was obedient to them, and that he "grew in wisdom and stature, and in favour with God and man" (v 51-52).

That Jesus *grew* is clearly very significant to Luke because he uses it to bookend his whole account of Jesus' childhood in Nazareth. Just before telling us about this visit to Jerusalem, he recounts that Mary and Joseph took him home to Nazareth as a baby and that "the child grew and became strong; he was filled with wisdom, and the grace of God was on him" (v 40). In Luke 1:80 we read largely the same thing about his cousin John, who also "grew and became strong in spirit". There was clearly something very unusual about Jesus, but at the same time something very normal. He grew like other children.

Jesus could claim God as his own Father, and he would demonstrate supremely in his death, resurrection and ascension that he had all the power and prerogatives of divinity. At the same time though, he grew. And not just physically—he grew in wisdom.

In other words, Jesus went to school. He had to learn his ABCs (or his *Alef Bet Gimels*—as it would have been in Hebrew). That may seem a bit counter-intuitive, given what we know about his identity. Indeed, the writer to the Hebrews marvels that "Son though he was he learned" (Hebrews 5:8). But learn he did.

Thinking about Jesus' mind is one of the best ways to get past our instinctive failure to take the reality of Jesus' humanity seriously. In the previous interlude we noted that some leaders in the early church had a hard time accepting Jesus' total divinity. Others had just as big a problem accepting his true humanity. And then, if you are anything like me, perhaps you are at risk of thinking about Jesus as a sort of mixture of divine and human, rather than as simultaneously being truly, fully, both. It's a natural mistake to make.

Christians struggled with this in the earliest days of the church too, and it led to all kinds of theological dead ends that had to be corrected. One such teaching was that of Apollinaris, Bishop of Laodicea, who died in 382 AD. He was an opponent of the Arian teaching which denied Jesus' divinity, and so proposed a way of understanding the incarnation that attempted to square the circle. His idea was that the Son of God essentially replaced the human mind and soul in the man Jesus. So Jesus was God in a human body (literally incarnate, "in flesh").

This is a really appealing idea in lots of ways, but

it's hard to see how a Jesus like that could really be called human in any real sense. Having a human mind seems to be quite an important part of life of most of us. In fact, a contemporary of Apollinaris, named Gregory, jibed that "if anyone puts his trust in him as a Man without a human mind, he is really bereft of mind, and quite unworthy of salvation. For that which [Christ] has not assumed He has not healed".[13] In other words, a Saviour without a human mind is only useful to humans without minds.

But Jesus *did* have a human mind. He learned; he grew in wisdom. Let that sink in. God cannot learn. But in Jesus, somehow, God became a learner.

Of course, this still leaves us with questions. Is it possible for a human mind to know in the way that God does? Surely not! He knows every movement of every subatomic particle in the universe from the beginning to the end of time; he knows the precise effects of each of those particles on each other and their relative position to each other at every conceivable moment in the history of matter; and he knows it all in one timeless moment of knowing. It melts my brain even to think about what it is like for God to think.

But if we try like Apollinaris to find a way of picturing what the incarnation is like, we end up in very deep and treacherous waters. Experience teaches that we do

---

13 Gregory of Nazianzen, "Letter to Cledonius the Priest: Against Apollinaris", in *A Select Library of the Nicene and Post-Nicene Fathers of the Christian Church*, Vol. 7, ed. Philip Schaff (T & T Clark, 1894), p 440.

better not to imagine the mechanism of the incarnation; instead, we should appreciate its mystery. Jesus Christ is truly and fully the Son of God. He made all things, and in him all things hold together. At the same time, he is, for the sake of our salvation, truly and fully a human being. He shared in our limitations, from the dust on his feet to the brain in his head. God has become one of us, for one reason and for one reason only: because he loves us, and wants to reconcile us to himself. "For God so loved the world that he gave his one and only Son, that whoever believes in him should not perish but have eternal life" (John 3:16).

Who can make sense of all this? Not me. As Jesus' friend Peter put it, "Even angels long to look into these things" (1 Peter 1:12). But while I may never fully comprehend how God came to put on his learner tags, I can marvel and wonder that he did. When it comes to our salvation, we all receive it like little children. There is a wisdom and an extremity of kindness in God's dealing with us that I will never fathom. But I can trust in it, and find rest.

4. GOD CAN'T BE SEEN

The writer Edgar Allan Poe wrote a short story called *The Purloined Letter*, in which a corrupt government minister steals a letter belonging to the queen and uses it for blackmail. The police's attempts to find the letter prove fruitless, despite checking behind the wallpaper and under the carpets of the minister's town house. No matter where they look, they cannot find it. An amateur detective, C. Auguste Dupin, manages to save the day by locating the stolen letter, looking rather tatty, in a nondescript letter rack. Knowing that the police would expect him to hide the letter, the minister had simply disguised it by turning the envelope inside out and writing a different address on it, and leaving it in plain sight.

Things can be invisible, or at least unseen, for lots of reasons. My car keys seem to have this extraordinary ability to make themselves selectively invisible. This power is most in evidence when I am in a rush and have already left it a bit too late to leave. In other words, sometimes I cannot see things because of what is going on inside me. At other times, I can't see things because the object in question is small or far away (especially as my eyesight gets worse). And there are other things I can't see because I am small and too close. The earth is a globe, but all my experience hides that from me, because I am small and near the ground. I don't see it because of scale.

I cannot see God. Neither can you. This is a universal human experience: "No one has ever seen God" (John 1:18). Indeed, one of the first people to get far away enough from the earth to see its curvature, Russian astronaut Yuri Gagarin, supposedly testified that even in space God was not visible.[14] Nor should we expect him to be: God is invisible, not for reasons of distance or proximity, or even of scale, but for a very different set of reasons.

The significance of God's invisibility is, like the purloined letter, hidden in plain sight in the Scriptures. It's stated clearly, but our eyes often skim past it. One interesting example is in Paul's first letter to Timothy. The letter is bookended by two expressions of praise to God. Both spring from the author's wonder at God's goodness to his people through the gospel of Jesus Christ, but his choice of words is very deliberate.

---

14 Gagarin is reported to have said "I don't see any God up here", but the phrase is not recorded in the flight logs and might have been attributed to him in a speech by the Soviet leader Nikita Khrushchev.

The first comes in chapter 1. As a way of stressing what really matters and is really central to the Christian life (and thus to the Christian ministry which Timothy has been tasked with renewing in Ephesus), Paul tells his own story of salvation: "I was once a blasphemer and a persecutor and a violent man," but God intervened: "Christ Jesus came into the world to save sinners—of whom I am the worst" (1 Timothy 1:13, 15). The recollection of God's grace is so powerful that Paul breaks off his argument to exclaim:

Now to the King eternal, immortal, invisible, the only God, be honour and glory for ever and ever. Amen.

(1:17)

These words are familiar to many of us, but they are a bit strange. As a child, I remember singing the famous hymn *Immortal Invisible*, and wondering why we were making so much fuss about God being invisible.

We find almost exactly the same pattern at the end of the letter. This time, Paul is writing about the second coming of Christ: "The appearing of our Lord Jesus Christ, which God will bring about in his own time" (6:14-15). Again, Paul breaks off in mid sentence to exclaim:

God, the blessed and only Ruler, the King of kings and Lord of lords, who alone is immortal and who lives in unapproachable light, whom no one has seen or can see. To him be honour and might for ever. Amen.

(6:15-16)

When we compare those two paragraphs, we can see that Paul is doing something more deliberate than simply spontaneously praying. He begins his letter with the first coming of Christ, followed by a prayer expressing some of God's attributes. He ends his letter talking about the second coming of Christ and then praises God for the same attributes again. This can't just be a coincidence.

So the question to ask is: why these attributes? After all, if I was going to sit down and write a list of five amazing things about God, I don't know that Paul's list in 1 Timothy 1 and 6 is what I would arrive at: King, yes; immortal, yes; honoured and glorious, yes! But invisible? It doesn't instantly make sense why Paul included that. That's what I mean when I say that God's invisibility is hidden in plain sight. When you read these verses, I imagine that, like me, you notice and pay attention to the obviously wonderful bits, and move straight past the invisibility without really noticing it. Which is sort of fitting I suppose.

But Paul *does* include it in his list. It seems only right to ask: "What is so praiseworthy about the fact that God cannot be seen?"

It is not just 1 Timothy that foregrounds the invisibility of God. Colossians 1:15, one of the greatest paeans of praise concerning Jesus Christ, begins: "The Son is the image of the invisible God". The writer to the Hebrews, seeking to strengthen his readers' commitment to Christ in a time of persecution, describes faith as "assurance about what we do not see" and reminds them that Moses' courage in leading the people out of Egypt stemmed from seeing by faith "him who is invisible" (Hebrews 11:1, 27). Perhaps the greatest literary achievement in the New Testament, John's prologue to his Gospel, ends as follows: "No one has ever seen God, but the one and only Son, who is himself God and is in the closest relationship with the Father, has made him known" (John 1:18).

One of the greatest writers in the early centuries of the church was the African theologian Origen (c.184 - c.253 AD). Reflecting on John's prologue, Origen wrote:

> John ... declares to all who are capable of understanding, that there is no nature to which God is visible: not as if He were a being who was visible by nature, and merely escaped or baffled the view of a frailer creature, but because by the **nature** of His being it is impossible for Him to be seen.[15]

In other words, God is genuinely invisible—it's not just that he's hidden or far away. Origen is not indulging in some obscure nit-picking intellectual exercise here. This comment is from his *De Principiis* ("On the First Principles"), which stands as the first systematic work of Christian theology. Like other similar works, it is "systematic" in that it sets out to expound the faith in a logical manner, so as to minimise confusion and error.

---

15 Origen, "De Principiis," in *The Ante-Nicene Fathers*, Vol. 4, ed. Alexander Roberts, James Donaldson, and A. Cleveland Coxe, trans. Frederick Crombie (Christian Literature Company, 1885), p 245. Emphasis mine.

And God's invisibility is so important and foundational that it made it into chapter 1.

But, you might still ask, *why* does belief in God's invisibility matter so much?

One way of thinking about that is to consider it from the perspective that we have begun to explore in previous chapters. In Scripture, we are presented with this one basic distinction, which is at the heart of reality: Creator and creature are different kinds of being. The Creator just "is"—he doesn't have a beginning, and he is not limited by anything in the creation. Creatures *do* have a beginning, and are constrained by the rules that underpin created reality—constraints like time and space. God, however, is unaffected and unlimited by time, and similarly by space.

As we saw in Psalm 139 in chapter 2, there is nowhere that God isn't. You can travel wherever you like—into space, to the depths of the sea, to the east, to the west—and you will find that God was there before you. This is connected to God's invisibility. He cannot be seen, because he does not have a body—as Jesus himself said when questioned about where God should be worshipped: "God is spirit" (John 4:24).

As you begin to really come to terms with what it means for God to be invisible and not have a body, you learn to relate to him differently. If he were a physical being, God would have a centre somewhere, and when we moved, it would either be towards or away from that centre. But God is not physical and thus he is able to be perfectly—that is, completely and without remainder—present everywhere. So as you sit and read this, all of God is present with you in the kitchen, or the park, or the bus, or the hospital room, or wherever you are. God is not divided up into parts. He is fully present to you. And because he is undivided, and not constrained by time and space, you also have—to put it in human terms—his full attention. God is not distracted, and you are not on the periphery of his thoughts.

That, I suspect, is either one of the most comforting, or the most unsettling, things that you have ever read. Every moment of your life is lived in the full glare of God's close attention. If you need comfort in the face of distress or injustice, you could do worse than reflect on this truth. God misses nothing. He is with you through all of it, and all accounts will be settled. On the other hand, if there are parts of your life that you are tempted to treat as "no go" areas for God, you might want to think again. Every moment of every day is lived, as some theologians put it, "*coram Deo*"—face to face with God. There is no room in your house, no moment in your day, no part of town, and indeed no town, in which God is not fully present.

That may seem counter-intuitive—in fact, it may be harder to swallow the better you know your Bible. From the days of Moses, God's presence went with his people in a visible way that was connected to the tabernacle, and later the temple. In that place, God's presence was visibly manifested in the Most Holy Place in such a way that anyone foolhardy enough to enter would die instantly. So was God somehow more "present" there than anywhere else?

Questions of God's presence (and indeed of the significance of "place") are multi-layered in the Bible and it would be easy to over-simplify and thus distort them. I won't attempt to give a complete account here. We should just note that God's presence can be talked about from our point of view and from God's. From our perspective, our experience of God's presence might change according to what he wants to *reveal* of his presence and where. From God's perspective (although it feels rather bold to speak in such terms), he is always and everywhere perfectly present.

So when you're lying awake, unable to sleep, looking around your room in the dim half-light of another dawn, you can remind yourself: God is here. Perfectly present. Immortal, invisible... and here. As perfectly present as the bedside lamp or the wardrobe or the heap of clothes in the corner—more so, in fact, because God's existence is the most real and because all of him is present everywhere. Which means that whether you're feeling fearful or frustrated or alone, you can take a deep breath, exhale slowly, and enjoy his presence.

It's worth spending a little bit of time, though, reflecting on the second reason that God is said to be invisible in Paul's first letter to Timothy. God "lives in unapproachable light" (1 Timothy 6:16). We've talked about what God *doesn't* have (a body) which means that he can't be seen. We need also to consider what God *does* have that also makes him invisible to us: glory. God is so blazingly pure and glorious that sinners like us cannot behold him.

The Old Testament repeatedly brings home the idea that seeing God is a dangerous thing. When "the angel of the LORD" appears to Manoah and his wife (parents of Samson), Manoah says, "We are doomed to die! ... We have seen God!" (Judges 13:22). Jacob, after his encounter with the same angel "called the place Peniel, saying, 'It is because I saw God face to face, and yet my life was spared'" (Genesis 32:30). When Moses asks God to reveal his glory, God says, "I will cause all my goodness to pass in front of you, and I will proclaim my name, the LORD, in your presence. I will have mercy on whom I will have mercy, and I will have compassion on whom I will have compassion. But ... you cannot see my face, for no one may see me and live" (Exodus 33:19-20).

So we're left with two complementary ideas. We are physically incapable of seeing God as he is. The human eye "sees" things when light bounces off the surface and reaches our eye. But God doesn't have a body with which to reflect light, so he cannot be seen. But we are also spiritually unable to see God—not because there is nothing to see, but because there is just too much. God doesn't reflect light, but he "dwells in unapproachable light". Trying to look at God is like trying to look at the sun. Indeed, trying to enter the fullness of God's presence would be more dangerous than trying to walk on the sun. In that sense, God's restraint in not manifesting his glorious presence fully on the earth, is just another aspect of his mercy. If he didn't protect us from his glory, we couldn't survive. That's another truth with which to occupy our minds on restless nights. How kind he is!

God is holy. Which, incidentally, gives us our next thing that God cannot do...

5. GOD CAN'T
BEAR TO LOOK

One TV show that the Tucker family loves to watch together is Richard Ayoade's *Travel Man: 48 hours in...* The premise is simple: Ayoade doesn't like to travel, and he takes a fellow comic or actor ("some of the most available and affordable names in light ent") away for a weekend to an iconic location. They cram as much as possible into 48 hours to answer the simple question: "We're here, but should we have come?" In order to make best possible use of the host's capacity for glib expressions of distaste, most of the visits seem to include opportunities to sample the least appetising of the local cuisine.

Recently, we watched his visit to Marrakech with actor Stephen Mangan. Their trip to a tannery was ok, because thankfully no one has yet brought the idea of smell-o-vision to the mass market. But when they ventured out to find street food, it produced visceral reactions amongst team Tucker. We watched through our fingers as a whole steamed sheep's head was piled onto a plate and the intrepid Mangan struggled to swallow brains, eyeballs, and lips, and keep them down. For our youngest it was all too much—he couldn't bear to watch at all.

Is God similarly squeamish? Not quite. But the Bible does tell us that sometimes, even he cannot bear to look. Habakkuk 1:13 says, "Your eyes are too pure to look on evil".

When it comes to sin and wrongdoing, God isn't even looking between his (metaphorical) fingers. He just can't stomach it at all. The second part of the verse in Habakkuk confirms this: "You cannot tolerate wrongdoing". It's not that God finds such things unpalatable or distressing—it's that he literally cannot even bear to look at them. That does not mean that he maintains a blissful ignorance, unaware of the evil going on in his world. We're told elsewhere that "the eyes of the LORD are everywhere, keeping watch on the wicked and the good" (Proverbs 15:3). Rather, the verse in Habakkuk highlights the strength of God's loathing of evil (rather than the extent of his knowledge of it). He cannot tolerate it even for a second. For the Christian, this is simultaneously enormously sobering and, in the end, profoundly comforting—although the comfort to be found here is at the end of a difficult and challenging journey.

In this chapter, we're going to go on that journey. It will take us through the story of the whole human race, written in the pages of the Bible over the course of about 1,500 years, and played out in the warp and woof of history and in the lives of countless human people. It's a journey that goes to the heart of your life and your story too. It traces the union with God that we were made for, and the separation we now experience from the God who cannot bear to look at evil.

The Bible begins with the one undeniable, non-negotiable, ultimate fact of reality: God himself. "In the beginning God..." (Genesis 1:1). It then describes his orderly, precise and beautiful creation of all other reality. This created order can exist only in dependence on, and in relation to, him.

The story of creation in Genesis 1 – 2 has a definite shape to it. The first six days are actually in three pairs, as God fills what he has formed: days one and four belong together (day and night; moon, sun and stars), as do two and five (sky and sea; birds and sea creatures), and three and six (land and vegetation; animals and human beings). God's work of creation culminates, on day six, with the creation of man and woman in God's own image. Their task is to bring creation to fullness by ruling "over the fish in the sea and the birds in the sky and over every living creature that moves on the ground" (1:28).

We often think of this as the climax of the story, but a better candidate for this role is actually the "rest" that God enjoys on the seventh day. Unlike the other days it has no pair. It also, curiously, lacks the "morning and evening" that describes each of the other days. The implication seems to be that the seventh day describes a permanent state of affairs. Rest is the goal of the creation.

The concept of the Sabbath—and of enjoying God's blessing as "rest"—is central to Scripture's account of what it means to live as God's people. Take, for example, the Ten Commandments. The fourth commandment is the only positive instruction about worship. The first three commands are actually negative in form: "You shall have no other gods before me ... You shall not make for yourself an image ... You shall not bow down to them or worship them ... You shall not misuse the name of the LORD your God" (Exodus 20:3-7). These commands preserve the unique dignity that belongs to God, highlighted by the distinction between Creator and created.

The command about the Sabbath is of a different kind: "Remember the Sabbath day by keeping it holy" (v 8). It requires that Israel, now set free from slavery in Egypt, shapes their entire pattern of life around observance of the Sabbath. Their working week will, for that reason, be six days long. Every seventh day, they are to act out the rest that God enjoyed when his work of creating was complete.

The significance of the concept of "rest" to the story of the Bible should not pass us by. Jesus' famous invitation in Matthew 11:28—"Come to me, all you who are weary and burdened, and I will give you rest"—is not an isolated saying simply addressed to the felt needs of his audience.

It picks up a thread that runs through the whole Old Testament. A few chapters on from Mount Sinai, Moses, at a point of crisis, is reassured by God that "my Presence will go with you, and I will give you rest" (Exodus 33:14). The settlement of the people in the promised land is described as "rest" at both the beginning and the end of the book of Joshua: "The LORD your God will give you *rest* by giving you this land" (Joshua 1:13) and "after a long time had passed and the LORD had given Israel *rest* from all their enemies around them, Joshua, by then a very old man, summoned all Israel" (23:1-2, emphasis mine, here and in any Bible quotes that follow).

In the New Testament, the writer to the Hebrews sees the promise of Sabbath-rest as being about more than just inheritance of a land or time off work, but as a promise of eternal life in God's presence:

> *For if Joshua had given them rest, God would not have spoken later about another day. There remains, then, a Sabbath-rest for the people of God; for anyone who enters God's rest also rests from their works, just as God did from his. Let us, therefore, make every effort to enter that rest, so that no one will perish by following their example of disobedience.*
>
> *(Hebrews 4:8-11)*

True rest, then, can only be found in the presence of, and by relationship to, the God who made us. That is why there is "no peace ... for the wicked" (Isaiah 48:22). As the great fourth-century theologian Augustine put it, "Lord you have made us for yourself, and our hearts are restless till they rest in you".[16]

Let's go back to the creation story, and its climactic picture of perfect rest: God and humanity in harmonious unity. This inevitably raises this question: if God made us to enjoy his rest, why are we so restless? We can't help but draw a contrast with the state of humanity today as we know it: a restless world, cut off from relationship with the God who cannot bear to look at evil. If God's plan in creating was to share his rest with his human creatures, what went wrong? And how can we get home?

So it is that, in Genesis 2, we are introduced to two particular trees in the Garden of Eden. One of these trees offers eternal life, the other a forbidden path to knowledge. It is the decision of the man and woman to take that forbidden path in Genesis 3 that explains the restless brokenness of the world. We do not inhabit the perfect place of rest God made us for, because he can't even bear to look at us. In fact, the whole of creation is restless, because the man and woman, crucial to the fulfilment of God's plan for his creation, have turned away from him. Their disobedience denied the truthfulness and power of his creative word,[17] and as such dismantled the fabric of creation.

---

16 Augustine, *Confessions*, ed. Michael P. Foley (Hackett Publishing Company, 2006), p 3. Language lightly updated.

17 The serpent's tempting of Eve invites her to believe that God's word is not true and thus lacks power ("You will not certainly die") and that it springs from unworthy motives on God's part ("God knows that when you eat of it your eyes will be opened, and you will be like God").

That alienation from God is the heart of our problem. Adam and Eve were cast out of Eden, the place of his rest. What the writer of Genesis does so brilliantly in telling us this story of our restlessness is to show us how serious our problem is. We cannot simply go back.

The rest of Scripture hums with this tension: God has made human beings in his own image—they are dear to him, and they have an innate loveliness and dignity; but they have chosen this path of rejection that alienates them from him and brings them into an apparently unresolvable conflict with his very character. Humans cannot see God and live. God cannot bear to look on the evils of humanity. So wherever God interacts with people, there is a burning question: how can this holy God live with unholy people? How can this tension be resolved? For most of Bible history, the best hope seems to be a complex dance of hiding and relationship.

So, in the Garden, in Genesis 3, Adam and Eve engage in a futile attempt to hide themselves from God (Genesis 3:10). This desire to hide from God is characteristic of human beings all the way through to the day of judgment: "They called to the mountains and the rocks, 'Fall on us and hide us from the face of him who sits on the throne'" (Revelation 6:16).

Indeed, even for God's holy people Israel, the dilemma remained real. The heart of the exodus story is not so much the departure from Egypt as it is the bringing of God's people into his presence: "I carried you on eagles' wings and brought you to myself," says God (Exodus 19:4). And yet, they can come so close, but no further. When the people arrive at Mount Sinai to receive the law, they are instructed not to come up the mountain where God's presence will be made manifest. In fact, Moses is solemnly warned: "Put limits for the people around the mountain and tell them, 'Be careful that you do not approach the mountain or touch the foot of it'" (v 12).

The climax right at the end of the book of Exodus is that God comes to dwell amongst his people (40:34-38). Half the preceding chapters are devoted to the design and building of the tabernacle that makes this meeting possible. The tabernacle—an elaborate tent, really—functions to keep God's people at a safe distance. The simultaneously glorious and terrifying conclusion of the book sees God's glory come down on the tent of meeting, but even "Moses could not enter the tent of meeting because the cloud had settled on it, and the glory of the LORD filled the tabernacle" (v 35).

The God who cannot be seen, and who cannot bear to look, found a way to be with his people. But in that very moment of triumph, the problem of their alienation is still plain in the great lengths that have had to be gone to in order to make such a meeting possible. But that was not the end of the story. We will return to this theme later.

For now, though, there is comfort even in the disturbing remembrance that God is not tame or indulgent. More than that, his judgment is utterly impartial; it is always perfectly right and fair.

This is so different from how we make judgments. The philosopher Bertrand Russell spoke of the idea of "emotive conjugation". It's a play on words that mimics the grammatical conjugation of an irregular verb. If you did French at school, you might have found yourself chanting things like: "Je vais, tu vas, il va"—I go, you go, he goes. Russell riffed off this pattern with an amusing observation that:

I am firm,
you are obstinate,
he is a pig-headed fool.

It has spawned many humorous imitations such as this, from a newspaper competition:

I am a concerned parent,
you tend to interfere,
she writes in her daughter's diary.

Or this, from the British political TV comedy, *Yes, Prime Minister*:

I give confidential press briefings;
you leak;
he's being charged under section 2A of the Official Secrets Act.

Whether or not you find those funny, the point is that we judge behaviour differently according to how we feel about the person in question. Our judgments about the world are full of bias and partiality. What we excuse in ourselves and minimize in those we respect, we condemn in those we dislike.

The statue of Lady Justice on top of the Old Bailey, the Central Criminal Court of England and Wales, wears a blindfold to symbolise her impartiality. Even so, we have to acknowledge that all human systems of justice tend to favour some over others. Some people have so much money that they can afford legal teams with enough resources to find every loophole in a case and string out court proceedings for so long that they tend to be able to win, even if it is just by attrition. Others, who rely on legal aid, are sometimes poorly represented. It's not always the case, but what was sadly true in Old Testament times remains true today: the widow and the orphan—that is, the dispossessed and resourceless—struggle to get justice. Maybe that's you right now.

And this is why it's good news that God cannot bear to look. God is so utterly, morally pure, so deeply committed to justice that it will "roll on like a river" with "righteousness like a never-failing stream" (Amos 5:24). One of the greatest pains of living in our broken world, especially for the disenfranchised poor, is that justice is so often not done. It will not always be so. God's complete inability to tolerate injustice or wrongdoing of any kind is a comfort and assurance to any who long to see the world put right. As the poet Henry Wadsworth Longfellow once put it:

Though the mills of God grind slowly;
yet they grind exceeding small;
Though with patience he stands waiting,
with exactness grinds he all.[18]

This is a great comfort when we are victims of injustice ourselves. God knows, and God cares. He wants justice, and he will bring it. So when you lie awake thinking about what has been done to you, you don't need to believe the lie that you don't matter, or that what has happened to you doesn't matter, or that you are not worthy of justice. God says that it does matter, and justice is right to pursue. Equally, if justice in this life is unlikely or impossible, you don't need to lie awake plotting a way to get revenge yourself, and nor do you need to sink into despair—God will most certainly bring justice, and perfect justice at that.

To those of us who are not on the receiving end of injustice, these are challenging truths. To know God's concern for righteousness should spur us to be people who seek to see justice done, particularly for those who lack the privilege to demand it for themselves. We can hardly claim to be devoted to God, who cannot bear to look at evil, if we are indifferent to it ourselves.

At the same time, though, God's concern for justice allows us to live at peace in a world of inequity. Because God cannot look on evil, he will not *overlook* evil either. One

---

18 "Retribution", *Poetic Aphorisms*, 1846; Longfellow was translating the work of earlier writers.

day, he will make all wrongs right and turn our upside-down world rightside up. We can sleep at night, knowing the end of the story; and we can rise in the morning, and seek to do what we can to put right the gut-churning wrongs that exist in even the best-governed societies.

INTERLUDE 3: GOD APPEARED

Sometimes a few words carry more meaning than a whole library of books. "Mr Gorbachev, tear down this wall" is a simple phrase, but it encapsulated a moment at which the end of the Cold War began to feel not only possible but real. Those words probably helped to bring about one of the most profound changes in global relations in all of history.[19]

---

19 The words "Mr Gorbachev, tear down this wall" were delivered by US President Ronald Reagan in a speech in West Berlin, given on 12th June 1987, in which called on the Soviet Union's leader Mikhail Gorbachev to open the Berlin Wall, which had divided East and West Berlin since 1961. Historians continue to argue

But that's nothing compared to the nine words (in Greek) that make up the fourteenth verse of John's Gospel: "The Word became flesh and made his dwelling among us" (John 1:14).

What a universe of meaning lies beneath those words. God himself, John tells us, through whom everything was made—the God who was there in the beginning—became flesh. God had dwelt with his people in the wilderness by means of the tabernacle, and later the Jerusalem Temple. But now God had come to dwell among them in an entirely new way: as one of them. God doesn't have a body and is invisible—but suddenly, there he was to be seen and touched. In fact, that's exactly the language John used to describe his own experience of Jesus when writing to believers in the early church: "That which was from the beginning, which we have heard, which we have seen with our eyes, which we have looked at and our hands have touched, *this* we proclaim" (1 John 1:1).

In chapter 4, we saw how Paul's first letter to Timothy was bracketed between two prayers of wonder at God's goodness. These mirrored each other, and both emphasised God's invisibility. Right in the middle of the letter, between those bookends, Paul lays out his chief concern for the church at Ephesus, where

---

over just how much difference the speech made. Nonetheless, the very fact that Reagan was able to say these words in that context at that moment, and that the wall did indeed come down, marked a massive shift in relations between the West and the Soviet East.

94

Paul had sent Timothy as his representative:

Although I hope to come to you soon, I am writing you these instructions so that, if I am delayed, you will know how people ought to conduct themselves in God's household, which is the church of the living God, the pillar and foundation of the truth. Beyond all question, the mystery from which true godliness springs is great:

He appeared in the flesh, was vindicated by the Spirit, was seen by angels, was preached among the nations, was believed on in the world, was taken up in glory.
(1 Timothy 3:14-16)

We can't possibly delve as deeply into these verses as I would like here. The vision of the church as God's household, with the exalted role of displaying his truth to the world, is exhilarating. But what I want you to notice here is simply the first thing Paul says about the "mystery" of the gospel: "He appeared".

At the heart of a letter which is hemmed in on both sides by exalted cries of praise and blessing to the invisible God, Paul states something that is so familiar that it might have lost its power to shock. The invisible God appeared. People saw him. The God who is so unimaginably great that he cannot *possibly* be seen, made himself visible. The God who is so unimaginably holy that he cannot *possibly* look on evil, lived amid the mess.

Why did he do this? It's actually there at the start of the letter—the fuel for Paul's first, fiery, prayer of worship: "Christ Jesus came into the world to save sinners" (v 15). The unapproachably glorious God became approachable, and visible, to rescue people like us—alienated and restless without him—and bring us home.

As if that wasn't enough, the letter ends with another "appearing", again in the context of a prayer of praise to the invisible God.

> *Keep this command*
> *without spot or blame*
> *until the appearing*
> *of our Lord Jesus*
> *Christ, which God*
> *will bring about in his*
> *own time—God, the*
> *blessed and only Ruler,*
> *the King of kings and*
> *Lord of lords, who*
> *alone is immortal*
> *and who lives in*
> *unapproachable light,*
> *whom no one has seen*
> *or can see. To him be*
> *honour and might*
> *forever. Amen.*
> *(6:14-16)*

So the whole letter—Paul's strategy for getting the erring Ephesian church back on track—is shaped around two appearings of the invisible God. Jesus Christ came into the world to save sinners; he will appear again, and that appearing will mean the end, and the new beginning, of all things.

These two appearings not only bracket the letter—they form the bookends to the era we now live in. They are the two fixed points in history between which it is possible to draw a straight line—a line that will show us how to make sense of our lives and how to live as the household of God. It can be hard to keep going in the Christian life. Sometimes the invisible God can seem absent from our experience—especially, as we saw in the last chapter, when we suffer injustice. Like the martyrs in Revelation 6, suffering Christians cry out, *How long, Lord?* (Revelation 6:10). But even when life is good, we struggle to keep living by faith and not by sight; to keep investing in God's kingdom rather than in the treasures of this earth. But Paul would want to reassure us: Jesus has appeared in history once already, as real and as solid as anything in front of you. And that is our guarantee that he will appear again—just as real and just as solid. More so, in fact. You're living on that straight line between his two appearings. He is coming soon.

And while we wait, we can take heart in who God is. Behind Christ's appearing is the unfathomable mystery of God's kindness and grace. In Jesus, God found a way to become small enough to find us in the darkness of our hiding places and lead us out into his otherwise unapproachable light.

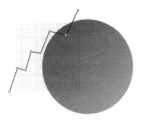

6. GOD CAN'T CHANGE

Perhaps one of the most dispiriting things anyone has ever said to me in an argument is, "I don't believe that you can really change". A statement like that really sucks the air out of the room. Once we stop believing that things can be different, the world feels like a pretty bleak place to be. In Dante's *Inferno*, the first poem in his three-part masterpiece, *The Divine Comedy*, he describes passing into hell through a gate under the inscription: "Surrender as you enter every hope you have".[20] I find it hard to imagine a better distillation of the essence of pure terror and anguish. To believe in the possibility of change is often what makes life bearable.

The iconic image of Barack Obama's wildly successful election campaign of 2008 was a poster, designed by the

---

20 Dante Alighieri, *The Divine Comedy*, trans. Robin Kirkpatrick (Penguin Classics, 2012, Kindle Edition), p 12.

artist Shepard Fairey, featuring a head and shoulders likeness of Obama and a single word: "hope". It carried the dynamic promise that things could be different—that this candidate could bring change.

As change is so important to us, we might not think it befits so great a being as God to say that he cannot change. After all, we almost always see change as a positive thing. I have come across a number of flowcharts like the one below. The point they make is obvious: if anything is unsatisfactory, change is the answer.

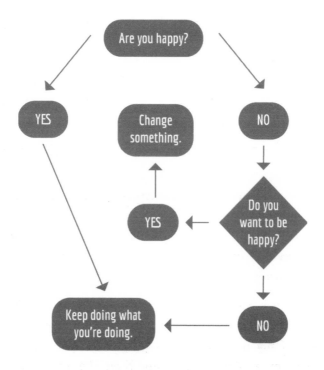

In a previous chapter we considered the fact that God can't change his mind. The focus of this chapter, however, is subtly but importantly different. Here we are considering not simply God's thoughts and words, but the very nature of his being. And while it might be a good thing that *we* can change, when we think about what God is like, we quickly realise it's a good thing that he can't. For instance, we read in 1 John 4:8 that "God *is* love". The only way that God could be "different" in that respect would be for him to somehow or to some extent *not be* love. This would feel like a pretty negative outcome, don't you think?

But don't worry—the whole point of this chapter is to affirm the fact that God cannot change. Back in the introduction, we took a brief look at God's self-identification as "I AM WHO I AM" (Exodus 3:14). Baked into the very name of God is this idea that everything that *is* true about God *has* to be true about him. As the uncreated Creator, he is defined by himself and not by another.

If we think about it from the perspective of what we have seen already, it seems pretty unlikely that God would change. After all, why would he? Just as before, we can approach this by distinguishing between external and internal reasons for change.

I'm sure you can think of at least a couple of ways that external factors produce change in you. For instance, the shape of my nose changed permanently, quite against my will, on a rainy Saturday one November in my early twenties. The cause of this change was a player from the opposing rugby team. A force greater than myself imposed facial re-ordering. I was powerless to resist.

A quite different kind of change, which was also initiated from the outside, came when I was a teenager, when a firefighter named Geoff spoke to a group of us in a classroom of a school in Devon. He explained how we were all on the wrong side of a spiritual chasm, which he drew on a diagram and labelled "sin". He told us that this rift between human beings and God was something we could never get across on our own. The change in me came when he placed a bridge on his diagram. It was in the shape of a cross, and he explained that Jesus died so that we can cross over and get to God.

I had grown up going to church. Faith has been in the family a long time. But as much as I wanted to "get it", nothing we did in services had really got through to me. I didn't understand, and I didn't really feel it—it was as if I was outside looking in. For example, at Christmas I was haunted by the thought that the angel's report of "peace on earth and goodwill to all people" at the birth of Jesus might have been somewhat overstated. Similarly, on Good Friday each year, all I had was a sense that the death of Jesus was something terrible and that Easter Sunday seemed like a pretty thin kind of happy ending to the story.

Suddenly, though, as Geoff spoke, it all swam into focus. The cross was not simply a tragedy, it was also a triumph. Jesus had died so that I could truly live. All at once, understanding and experience came flooding in. The Christian faith—to which I had felt like an uncomprehending outsider—made sense at last. And with prayer, I felt like an insider too: he was now my Jesus. He had died for me and through him I had a new relationship with the God who made me.

That was real change for me, and it came not through force, but through ideas (although that's not to deny the Spirit's role in the event). As I received new information, my mind, and also my heart, were changed—every bit as much as my nose.

So change comes to us either against our will, by force, or by changing our will—by way of new information or ideas. This, in fact, is one of the wonderful things about becoming a Christian: in the power of the Spirit, we really *can* change.

But God? Not so much.

As we have already seen, as the uncreated Creator, God has no rival. There is nothing that exists, other than himself, that he did not make. For that reason, there isn't anything that has power even remotely comparable to his, let alone superior. If God had a nose, no one would be able to rearrange it for him against his will. God cannot be forced by external factors.

You will remember, also, that there is not much chance of God changing because of new information or ideas. We have already established that God can't change his mind, so God is not going to be changed from the outside by having his mind changed. There is no new information, or arrangement of information, that could alter his course.

This just leaves the possibility of change from within. Could God ever change because of an "internal" reason? Part of the answer to this lies in the next chapter—God cannot suffer. After all, the prime motivation for change lies in a sense that something is not right. When it comes to God himself, he is most profoundly unlike us in that he is perfect in every conceivable way. There is no possibility of change for the better. Any change in God would be change for the worse. So he doesn't choose change, as it would be negative if he did. And since he is already perfect, he doesn't have any flaws that would cause him to pursue change for the worse.

But so what? Is all this just a kind of theological navel gazing? Why should we concern ourselves with a question like this?

The ways that Scripture speaks to us about God's changelessness makes that clear. Take, for example, Psalm 102:

> *25 In the beginning you laid the foundations of the earth,*
>   *and the heavens are the work of your hands.*
> *26 They will perish, but you remain;*
>   *they will all wear out like a garment.*
>   *Like clothing you will change them*

> *and they will be discarded.*
> [27] *But you remain the same,*
> *and your years will never end. (Psalm 102:25-27)*

The psalmist takes the most ancient and enduring aspects of the creation, "the foundations of the earth, and the heavens" (v 25), and compares them to God: the latter is permanent, the former is not. Even the most impressive of natural features, such as, say, the Grand Canyon, is impermanent and subject to change, if viewed on a long-enough timescale. The Grand Canyon, of course, would not be as it is but for the slow process of erosion by the Colorado River. Even the heavenly bodies like the sun, moon, and stars, are merely temporary lights that will eventually burn themselves out—"they will all wear out like a garment" (v 26).

It is not natural, then, for us to conceive of anything as properly permanent, but God insists that this is how we think of him. He is unlike anything in the creation because whilst everything else changes and eventually wears out like clothing, "[he remains] the same, and [his] years will never end".

Knowing this should move us to wonder at God's greatness. He is so great that he can only be known by faith. He is so beyond any earthly categories that it is only as he reveals himself to us that we can even begin to see him as he is. That seems to be a lesson that we keep coming back to, doesn't it? And rightly so—it is the beginning of knowing God, to recognise his surpassing greatness.

But the psalmist has a further end in view as he reflects on God's unchanging being: he concludes, "The children of your servants will live in your presence; their descendants will be established before you" (Psalm 102:28). Here is a foundation that you can build your life on that will never fail. The God who always endures and is always the same can establish your life securely and that of generations to come. In a changing world, it is a wonderful thing to know an unchanging God.

Isaiah makes a similar point, in the section that comes just before the passage we considered in the first chapter:

> *⁶ A voice says, "Cry out."*
> *And I said, "What shall I cry?"*
> *"All people are like grass,*
> *and all their faithfulness is like the*
> *flowers of the field.*
> *⁷ The grass withers and the flowers fall,*
> *because the breath of the LORD blows on them.*
> *Surely the people are grass.*
> *⁸ The grass withers and the flowers fall,*
> *but the word of our God endures for ever."*
>
> *(Isaiah 40:6-8)*

This time, the comparison is between God's permanence and the tragic impermanence of human beings. People are "like grass" in that they quickly fade from the earth and cannot ultimately deliver on their promises—"their faithfulness is like the flowers of the field" (v 6). But God's promises are of a different order. Just as God can be trusted not to fade or fail, so, Isaiah tells us, can his word. When God speaks, that word is unchanging and permanent too.

Although it might not feel like it, printed on flimsy paper as it probably is, your Bible is the one thing you own that will last for ever. Not the physical book, sure—in fact, my dog once ate my favourite Bible. But as we read God's word, we find ourselves in contact with permanence in a way that is not true of anything else in our experience. To some extent, even the laws of nature are changeable in comparison to God's laws, as they reflect the nature of a changing reality. It is hard for us to imagine, but in the words God has spoken to his people, we encounter something that will outlast everything any human civilisation has ever achieved. God's words will outlast even the sun whose warming rays caused the trees to grow on whose paper it is printed.

Perhaps that helps to refresh your perspective on reading and studying the Bible. It can be easy, if you've been a Christian for a while, to see reading God's word as something you *should* do, but secretly to feel little enthusiasm for it. But in a world of uncertainty, insecurity and impermanence, we are offered access to wisdom and truth that will never change and will always be relevant. Civilisations come and go, nations rise and fall, "but the word of our God stands for ever" (v 8).

And the message that it brings us of its author is that his stability is our basis for security in a world of insecurity. Speaking through Malachi, God says:

"I the LORD do not change. So you, the descendants of Jacob, are not destroyed. Ever since the time of your ancestors you have turned away from my decrees and have not kept them. Return to me, and I will return to you," says the LORD Almighty. (Malachi 3:6-7)

God is so faithful that even in the face of the fickleness of his people he continues to bear with them and to call them back to himself. That word "So" in verse 6 is precious. God does not change, and "so"—for *that* reason—Jacob is not destroyed. God's promises never fail.

It may be that you are reading this book at a time in your life where you are wandering away from God. I know the feeling! And if you are like me, realising that fact can be crushing, because you fear that you could lose your grip entirely, or that maybe you already have. That's not how it works though. As Asaph says in Psalm 73, speaking of his own struggles with doubt, and the temptation to give up: "My flesh and my heart may fail, but God is the strength of my heart and my portion forever" (Psalm 73:26). Our security is not in ourselves and in our own ability to keep going with God. It is in God's faithfulness to his promises. If you are wandering, or have wandered, God's word continues to hold true: "Return to me, and I will return to you" (Malachi 3:7). He won't abandon you!

This brings us to one final passage in the Bible that speaks of God's unchanging nature, this time from the New Testament:

Don't be deceived, my dear brothers and sisters. Every good and perfect gift is from above, coming down from the Father of the heavenly lights, who does not change like shifting shadows. He chose to give us birth through the word of truth, that we might be a kind of firstfruits of all he created. (James 1:16-18)

Again, we find God compared with the highest elements of creation—the heavenly bodies. The sun casts shadows of different lengths during the day, the stars seem to move around in the sky, but the God who made them is not like them. The point James is making here is that, no matter what happens, we should not doubt God's goodness towards us. His readers were facing all kinds of challenges, suffering and persecution, and were beginning to wonder whether God was really *for* them.

Perhaps that is a temptation that you, too, have faced. So many difficult and painful things happen in this broken world that it can be easy to think that maybe God doesn't actually like us very much. We can find ourselves believing that when things go well it is a sign that God is pleased with us, and when they go badly we ask, "What did I do wrong?" Our sense of whether God really wants to bless us rises and falls with our circumstances.

James, though, will have none of it. God doesn't change like that. His love is not fickle and his plan for your life is certain. That's what it means when it says that "he chose to give us birth through the word of truth, that we might be a kind of firstfruits of all he created" (v 18). God called you to himself with the end in mind. The beginning—new birth— is a sign that God intends to take us all the way through to the end as "a kind of firstfruits of all he created".

My life is full of unfinished projects: things I began but never quite saw through. I have a purple belt in Ju Jitsu, but not a black belt. I just couldn't find the right club to join when we moved cities. I have grade 5 on the trumpet, but never got to grade 8, because I got braces on my teeth in my teens and took a "break" from learning, but never got back to it. I know what it is to start, but fail to finish. Thank God that he is not like me. He never started something and failed to finish it. His beginnings all reach their intended goal, and so it will be for all his people, because he "does not change like shifting shadows". What a relief!

In F.H. Lyte's great hymn *Abide with me*, there is a beautiful line that captures the comfort of God's unchanging nature brilliantly:

Change and decay in all around I see,
O thou who changest not, abide with me.

As you draw the curtains and lay down, weary after another day in a world of change and chance, we can make those words our prayer, and sleep secure in the knowledge that it will always be answered.

7. GOD CAN'T BE LONELY

"**N**o man is an island entire of itself," wrote the 17th-century poet John Donne. To which, some 400 years later, the comedian Robin Williams added: "But some are peninsulas". They both have a point—hard as we might try, human beings cannot ever be totally independent. We are made for relationship.

This is true from the very first moment that we draw breath. Babies don't just need to be cared for physically—they need to be loved if they are to thrive. In her book *Why Love Matters*, Sue Gerhardt explains what happens to human beings who do not experience positive social interactions, especially in the first two years of life. Whilst we might not be surprised to learn that a child's emotional and mental development can be affected by a lack of relationship, the same is true of their physical bodies. One distressing piece of evidence that Gerhardt cites is the case of Romanian orphans in a children's home, who were kept safe, well fed and warm, but who were otherwise left alone. Gerhardt writes: "Those who were cut off from close bonds with an adult by being left in their cots all day, unable to make relationships, had a virtual black hole where their orbitofrontal cortex should be".[21] Part of their brains just had not developed.

No one can flourish—in fact, no one can be fully themselves—without other people. Most of us in the West tend to think of ourselves as individuals who then form relationships as we choose, but the reality is somewhat different. There is no "ourselves", at least not in the fullest sense, without relationship. In other words, it's not just that we *have* relationships: we *need* them. Our relationships are part of who we are. That's why, when we lack meaningful relationships, we feel lonely. Loneliness is a genuine and deepening problem in our society—and perhaps it's a genuine and deepening problem for you, personally.

This raises some interesting questions when it comes to God. Are relationships essential for him? On the face of it, to say that "God can't be lonely" might suggest that they aren't. After all, humans suffer loneliness when they lack relationships, because relationships are an expression of our fundamental nature. To say that God *cannot* be lonely suggests that relationships function differently for him. Indeed, a God who cannot be lonely might just be forbiddingly aloof: cold and unrelational.

---

21 Sue Gerhardt, *Why Love Matters* (Brunner-Routledge, 2004), p 38.

While we'll see that this last part is, thankfully, not the case, God's lack of loneliness is a vital expression of his independence from the creation. God doesn't *need* what he has made to complete some aspect of himself that would otherwise be unfulfilled. To deny this would be to risk "deifying" the universe: that is, if God cannot be fully himself without the creation, then in some way the universe is *necessary* to God and therefore somehow on a par with him. If we were to accept this, we would find ourselves at odds with God's revelation of himself: "I am who I am" (Exodus 3:14). His existence is not subject to a changing creation—in fact, we saw in an earlier chapter that even when it comes to knowing the creation, he is not reliant on the creation. Rather, the creation couldn't exist unless he knew it.

If his independence from the creation was all we knew of God, then to talk about having a relationship with him—as Christians do—would be a very odd thing indeed. The Greek philosophers such as Aristotle concluded that there must be a "first cause" behind the universe—that is, a god—but thought that such a divine being would be too distant to be knowable. Ancient Christian heresies frequently revealed the influence of this kind of thinking. The Arians of the fourth century, who denied that Jesus could truly be divine, did so in part because of his contact with created things. They just didn't think it possible that such a distant, independent God could enter his creation in this way.

Similarly, a natural question raised by a contemporary religion like Islam, whose deity seems to be naturally as alone as the god of the Greeks, is, "How could a relationship with God be possible?" Any relationship Allah has with creatures must, it seems, be out of character. Whereas, for humans, love is an inescapable necessity, if a god existed entire and alone outside of time before creation, then it cannot be so for them.

Therefore, any relationship one might have with such a being would not be something that comes naturally. Love cannot possibly be an expression of their nature, as love inherently involves giving to another. In that sense, any love a god like this might show to us is a posture, not an expression of who they are. In fact, it becomes hard to genuinely conceive of such a being as a "who" rather than an "it", since to be a personal subject as we understand it is to be relational by nature.

Yet, as we open the pages of the New Testament, we find ourselves confronted with these extraordinary words: "God is love" (1 John 4:8). If we are to take this seriously, then we must conclude that relationship is every bit as central to the identity of God as it is to human beings. When we consider that human beings are made in the image of God, that may be unsurprising, but in the world of genuinely monotheistic religions it is dynamite.

So we're left with a tension: how can God be truly God— that is, truly independent—and yet also relational down to the very core?

The same John who wrote "God is love" wrote his Gospel account of the life of Jesus with that mystery at its heart. From the book's opening line—"In the beginning was the Word, and the Word was with God, and the Word was God" (John 1:1)—to its epilogue, John wants us to know something very specific about Jesus. He sums it up like this:

Jesus performed many other signs in the presence of his disciples, which are not recorded in this book. But these are written that you may believe that Jesus is the Messiah, the Son of God, and that by believing you may have life in his name. (20:30-31)

John doesn't simply want us to know that Jesus is divine—that is, that he is God and thus able to be our Saviour and rightly to be worshipped. John's intention is actually more focused than this; he wants us to believe that Jesus is "*the Son* of God". Perhaps you can already begin to see why he puts things so precisely.

This idea that Jesus is truly divine and also in relationship with the divine is the central insight of the Christian faith that sets it apart from any other system of belief that has ever been put forward amongst human beings. Think again of John's opening line: "The Word was God, and the Word was with God". That one sentence comes laden with world-changing meaning.

In speaking of Jesus in this way, John reveals a God who can make sense of our human experience whilst upholding the understanding of God revealed in the Old Testament—as one who is independent and self-existent. God, like us, cannot exist without love, but that love is not dependent on any other being because he exists eternally in relationship. God could never be lonely because he is in himself never alone; he is three, not only one. He is Trinity.

In the life, death, resurrection, and ascension of the Lord Jesus Christ, we are offered a breathtaking glimpse of the reality of God himself, who exists as Father, Son and Holy Spirit in eternal and unbreakable relations of love. God's Trinitarian nature has a number of consequences for the way we see God, ourselves and the world around us.

First of all, we have a God who not only can love but who does so as an expression of his very nature. God is love, and as Trinity, he expresses love in its fullness. The medieval theologian Richard of St Victor observed that as three, God can be fulfilled in love not only between two persons, but also in two expressing a shared love of a third.[22] In a world that we cannot either comprehend or inhabit without significant relationships, here is a God who can make sense of it all.

Not only so, but this God can offer to even the most alienated and alone amongst us the possibility of true relationship—one that can be trusted, and that can restore and heal us at our deepest place of need. As the introduction to John's Gospel goes on to say: "To all who

---

22 See Richard of St Victor, *De Trinitate*, especially Book V.

did receive [Jesus the Son of God], to those who believed in his name, he gave the right to become children of God—children born not of natural descent, nor of human decision or a husband's will, but born of God" (John 1:12-13). The Father really is a father, and—as unthinkable as this might sound to anyone who has begun to get hold of what it means for God to be God—he can be *our Father*. This is not a *stance* that God takes towards his people. He is, at heart, a Father.

Another picture that God frequently uses in the Bible to describe his relationship to his special people can help us to get our heads around this: that of the bridegroom to his bride. That is the language that John the Baptist used of Jesus: "The bride belongs to the bridegroom. The friend who attends the bridegroom waits and listens for him, and is full of joy when he hears the bridegroom's voice. That joy is mine, and it is now complete" (John 3:29). The apostle Paul also uses this metaphor, and immediately quotes from Genesis 2:24: "For this reason a man will leave his father and mother and be united to his wife, and the two will become one flesh" (Ephesians 5:31). In other words, the relationship between Jesus and his church is so like the relationship between a bride and groom to the extent that it renders them genuinely *one*.

Now, don't miss the significance of this: to be united to the Son means that we come to share in a relationship not only to him, but to his Father. To be united to the one who is by nature *Son* means that we can share his prerogative of calling God *Father*. To be a Christian is actually to be swept up into the eternal relations of love between the Father and the Son. Can you even begin to comprehend the enormity of that? No wonder Paul immediately responds to his own metaphor by saying, "This is a profound mystery" (Ephesians 5:32).

It is indeed! If you are a Christian, then the closest thing God can find to tell you how he feels about you is the look on a bridegroom's face when his bride appears at the bottom of the aisle on their wedding day. The love God has for each one of his people is the love that has always existed between the Father and the Son in eternity. We live in a culture that is obsessed with romantic relationships. We are conditioned to believe that the solution to the longing for connection we feel is to make sure that we do not go to bed alone. But the Christian goes to sleep and wakes again under the comforting gaze of their Father God.

A second consequence of God's Trinitarian nature is that it causes us to reflect on what is most central to who we are as humans. We live at a time when "identity" and "authenticity" are hugely significant and contested ideas. That we should devote time and energy to discovering who we are and being "true to ourselves" is pretty much inarguable in Western culture in the 21st century. At the same time, the level of confusion and anxiety about those same ideas has soared. But what if in looking at ourselves, we're looking in the wrong place? What if my life cannot make sense without a network of interdependent relationships? What if authentic humanity lies not so much in self-actualisation as it does in a commitment to other-person-centred, self-giving love?

When we grasp this, it makes a huge difference. I remember one evening several years ago, when the phone rang as we were celebrating my wife's birthday. It was about 10pm and the voice at the other end of the phone asked if I was the minister. I excused myself from the gathering of people and entered my study. The voice continued: "Will God forgive me if I kill myself?" Now, that was not a question that I thought it would be good to answer, so I asked questions instead. The conversation developed and went on for some time. We agreed to meet the next morning.

It was a long and, in some ways, painful meeting. Some of the things my new friend described as having happened in her life were heartbreaking to hear. But the worst thing was her sense that, as a result of these things, her life was empty—not least because she felt so broken and unable to do things. She was a believer, but she felt useless, with nothing to offer. So she had concluded that she was a waste of space and resources.

As she shared her story, and her struggle to love and honour God in the midst of it all, I became profoundly aware of what a privilege it was to be sitting with her. Here was a dearly loved child of God, setting me an example of faith in the face of griefs I could not really imagine. The conversation moved to the way that God has set things up in such a way that we need each other in relationship. It's not just a matter of what we can do for each other, but that we find the truest expression of Christian discipleship in lives of self-giving, other-person-centred love. In that sense, just by letting people in the church love her, my friend could do something of great value.

Now, I am not so naïve as to think that mental-health struggles can simply be solved by being told to see the world differently. In the situation that I just described, we worked with the local mental-health team, and I didn't get off the phone on that first evening until I knew that there were people in this lady's home and that she was safe in that moment of crisis. But, at least in part from our conversation, change did follow in the months ahead. She was prepared to risk engaging with people, and became part of our church. Gradually, she started to accept the possibility that her value was not found in what she did, but in relationship—primarily with God and by extension with his people. Things genuinely got better, and I continue to thank God for all that he taught me through her, and for the deep and genuine blessing it was for me to know her during my years serving in that church family.

It's good news that God cannot be lonely. He exists in a network of perfectly fulfilled relationships, and as such, we see that such relationships of love must also be central to true human identity. The way to find yourself is in giving yourself to others. It is when we take ourselves out of the centre that we become our truest selves. In a world that lies awake fretting over questions of identity, the Christian can sleep well in the shadow of the God who is love. And on our loneliest nights—when bereavement or heartbreak has left us utterly bereft—this is where we can turn to for comfort. To belong to God is to be caught up in self-giving, other-person-centred love.

8. GOD CAN'T SUFFER

There is a relatively rare syndrome (estimated to occur in roughly 1 in every 25,000 people) called Channelopathy-associated Congenital Insensitivity to Pain (CIP), which, if you are unfortunate enough to have it, means that you cannot feel pain at all.

At first, it might seem strange to describe people with this syndrome as unfortunate. But as Claire Resuggan, whose son Tyler has CIP, told one newspaper, it's a nightmare: "Some people think it sounds great not feeling pain, it's actually dreadful and life-threatening".[23] By the age of eight, Tyler had visited the Accident and Emergency Department 27 times and fractured a bone for every year of his life, including his skull. It might not surprise you

---

23 Candice Fernandez "Real-life superhero: The boy who can't feel pain", *New Zealand Herald*, 8 May, 2017. https://www.nzherald.co.nz/lifestyle/real-life-superhero-the-boy-who-cant-feel-pain/CPSZIL5KCQ43G4PF7XPIICEVNE/ (accessed 1 Dec 2020).

to learn that though the condition is rare in children, it is even more rare in adults.

Pain is a horrible thing. I have friends whose chronic pain has reduced their capacity to take part in everyday life to almost nothing. Yet pain is also a vital part of life. Without it, we are left vulnerable and exposed. The capacity to feel pain is a good thing for human beings to have—even if the benefit lies largely by learning to flee it. Pain seems, ironically, to be something that is essential to human flourishing in the fallen world that we're in.

But imagine for a moment trying to explain the debilitating experience of something as simple as toothache to someone like Tyler, who can put their hand in a pan of boiling water without discomfort. How would you describe it? It's hard for any of us to understand something which we have no capacity to experience. How can someone who cannot suffer even begin to imagine what it's like to be in pain?

Therefore, to say—as the title of this chapter does—that God cannot suffer, will, when we stop to think about it, leave us with some questions. If God is unable to suffer, does that mean he is unable to understand our pain? How can he care if he doesn't know what it's like? We might start to imagine that God is monstrously indifferent to our suffering.

Such a view of God is not only unpalatable, it's deeply unbiblical. In the Scriptures we find a God who describes his relationship to his people in these terms:

Can a mother forget the baby at her breast and have no compassion on the child she has borne? Though she may forget, I will not forget you! (Isaiah 49:15)

This is hardly a picture of a cold, unfeeling deity. God invites his readers to imagine the most intensely protective and compassionate scene they can—a mother feeding her baby—and insists that his own care for his people is deeper, more heartfelt, and more reliable. And every mother—including Tyler's—knows what it is to suffer on behalf of her child.

Given that, it may surprise you that for almost the entire history of the church, there has been near unanimous agreement that God cannot suffer. During the early centuries of Christianity, all orthodox theologians and even most of their heretical opponents agreed that God was, to use the theological term, "impassible"—unable to suffer. At the first four ecumenical councils[24]—at which the basic definitions of Christian beliefs, the Creeds, were hammered out—God's impassibility was one of the ideas which boundaried all discussion about the incarnation of the Son of God.

Fast forward a millennium or so to the doctrinal statements of the Reformation, and there too impassibility was included as a fundamental characteristic of God's being. For instance, both the Anglican *39 Articles* and the

---

24 Nicaea in 325 AD, Constantinople in 381 AD, Ephesus in 431 AD, and Chalcedon in 451 AD.

Westminster Confession describe God as "without body, parts or passions".[25] It's the "passions" bit we're interested in here. ("Im-passible" means "without passions"). In the 21st century we tend to think of a "passion" as something positive, but it derives from the Latin word for suffering, and at that time generally referred to an emotional response that controls and masters you.

So, for almost all of church history there has been a basic consensus that God cannot suffer. How could Christians in days gone by insist on something that seems so counter-intuitive to us?

In thinking about that question, we should remember that theology, if done in submission to divine revelation, *is* a profoundly counter-intuitive pursuit. We instinctively tend to measure God against ourselves, so as we encounter a God who is in many ways radically unlike us, we have to keep dismantling the mental images we keep assembling of what he might be like. As he says through the prophet Isaiah, "'For my thoughts are not your thoughts, neither are your ways my ways,' declares the LORD. 'As the heavens are higher than the earth, so are my ways higher than your ways and my thoughts than your thoughts'" (Isaiah 55:8-9). When it comes to theology, if it's not sometimes uncomfortable, you're not doing it right.

---

25 *39 Articles of Religion* (1562), Article 1; *Westminster Confession of Faith* (1646), Chapter II, Article 1.

We should also remember that God's inability to suffer was not, for our Christian forebears, an idea independent of or disconnected from everything else they believed to be true about him. You can see it in that phrase from the English confessions above, "without body, parts or passions". Just as God doesn't relate to space in the same way that we do (he has no body), his emotional life is not like ours either.

Perhaps it might help you to think about it like this: how can a timeless being suffer? Suffering generally involves a response to something that happens to you. As we observed when we thought about how God cannot learn, God does not sit inside the world of space and time like we do and respond to things that happen. He exists in a different way, but he relates to every moment of time and space perfectly and all at once.

To put it another way, maybe you remember our discussion of "perfection" as a way of describing God, right back in the first chapter. If not, let me refresh your memory. As Creator of all, God is the source of every good thing. There is therefore no good thing that he lacks, and he cannot be improved on by adding or taking anything away. As such, he is completely independent of the creation—he doesn't "need" it. He shapes it, but it doesn't shape him.

A "passion", as conceived of theologically, is not identical to an emotion; rather, it refers to a response that controls you. If the creation can produce an unwilled response in God himself, then, in some way and to some extent, he is subject to the creation at that point; it has power over him. In that case, there is a lot at stake in the question of whether or not God can suffer. To say that he is capable of it may seem fairly inconsequential, but in fact it raises some very big questions about God's being.

It's vital to understand that to speak of God as impassible is not the same as to say that he is apathetic. He may not have passions, but he certainly has *com*passion. God is not indifferent to either our sin or our suffering. So, we mustn't emphasise God's impassibility to the extent that we neglect everything else the Bible says about him. God's relationship to us is described in creaturely terms so that we can understand. We must not forget that he tells us that our rebellion grieves him (Psalm 78:40), our repentance delights him (Luke 15:10), and our neediness moves him to pity (Psalm 72:12-14). As the great Princeton theologian Charles Hodge wrote:

> *The Scriptures do not mock us when they say, "Like as a father pitieth his children, so the Lord pitieth them that fear Him." (Psalm 103:13.) He meant what He said when He proclaimed Himself as "The LORD, the LORD God, merciful and gracious, long-suffering and abundant in goodness and truth." (Exodus 34:6.)*[26]

---

26 Charles Hodge, *Systematic Theology*, vol. 1 (Logos Research Systems, Inc., 1997), p 429. It is vital to observe that Hodge was completely committed to the "Classical" doctrine of God which includes the idea of impassibility. He wrote in the same volume: "To the divine essence, which in itself is infinite, eternal, and unchangeable, belong certain perfections revealed to us in the constitution of our nature and in the word of God. These divine perfections are called attributes as essential to the nature of a divine Being, and necessarily involved in our idea of God," p 368.

Given that, is it possible that the Church Fathers were wrong in their insistence that God can't suffer? Several modern thinkers have argued as much. In recent times (by which I mean, since the mid-19th century!), it has become popular to charge the early theologians of the church with introducing unbiblical "Greek" ideas about God into the Christian tradition. These are said to have endured right up until the more "enlightened" approach of those who could look back and identify where the error crept in. The impassible God of the early theologians, it is argued, has more in common with Aristotle's "unmoved mover"—a being so remote from the creation as to be completely untouched and untouchable—than with the compassionate God of the Bible.

The problem with this particular theory, as with so many totalising theories that offer a simple explanation of "the past", is that it works brilliantly as long as you ignore the evidence. The early theologians of the church whose work has been preserved argued from Scripture, and though they sometimes used the language of Greek philosophy, this was to enable clarity and precision in theological discussion. So even a theologian like Tertullian (c.160-230 AD), who was so allergic to Greek philosophy that he once asked, "What has Athens to do with Jerusalem?", was strongly committed to impassibility. Basing his argument on Exodus 3:14 ("I AM WHO I AM"), he wrote, "Deity has its origin neither in novelty nor in antiquity, but in its own true nature. Eternity has no time. It is itself all time. It acts; it cannot then suffer."[27] And this is why a God who has no passions can nonetheless show compassion; whereas passions are an uncontrolled response to an external event, compassion is an expression of God's internal (and eternal) being. It's not that God doesn't "feel" (if we can use that word)—it's that what God "feels" flows from his character; it isn't forced on him from something outside of himself. In this sense, he does not *suffer* (a word which comes from the Latin "to bear" or "undergo").

The early Christians—even the most fiercely anti-philosophical ones such as Tertullian—knew God to be supremely and unchangeably *blessed*—that is, perfectly fulfilled in every good thing. In other words (and at the risk of over-simplifying), he is as happy as it is possible to be. How then could he suffer?

This idea of God being supremely blessed certainly did not originate with the Greeks—it was derived directly from God's revelation of himself in the Bible. As you may know, the covenant name of God was considered so holy by the Jews of Jesus' day that it could not be spoken aloud. Hence the high priest asks Jesus in Mark 14:61, "Are you the Messiah, the Son of *the Blessed One*?" To speak of God as the "blessed one" was so well established that only God himself is described as "blessed" in the New Testament.[28]

---

27 Tertullian, "The Five Books against Marcion," in *The Ante-Nicene Fathers*, Vol. 3, ed. Alexander Roberts, James Donaldson, and A. Cleveland Coxe, trans. Peter Holmes (Christian Literature Company, 1885), p 276.

28 The Greek word here is "eulogetos" and should not be confused with "makarios",

So when we talk about God not being able to suffer, what we are really talking about is God's identity as "the blessed one"—the being who is the source of all good things and who does not lack anything.

Now, even with all that said, we're still left with lots of questions: questions about how God relates to this broken world, and how we can say that he understands and cares about our suffering even whilst saying that our suffering does not challenge his blessedness. Yet, as with so many other things, there must be a point at which we stop and accept that there are some things we will never understand. That's not to suggest that we have reached that point here! There is still much more that can be said about the subject. But I fear that this would become a very different kind of book if I tried to press further into the detail.

For now, what I really want to suggest is that, even if it doesn't initially feel like it, God's impassibility is supremely good news and should comfort you as you lay your head on your pillow at night.

In the first instance, it is surely a relief to be reminded once again, and to see from another angle, that God really is able to keep his promises. Grief and suffering is an unavoidable experience for any person who lives in this broken world. There is no shame in that—the Psalms are

---

which is the word Jesus uses in the Beatitudes and is often rendered as blessed in English translations.

full of heartfelt and full-throated expressions of lament. Yet, I can think of times in my life when such "passions" have made it impossible for me to fulfil my responsibilities. The obvious one would be the sudden death of my brother, in the immediate aftermath of which I could barely stand up, let alone fulfil my work commitments for the day. In God's case, though, there is nothing in all creation that can deflect him from his purposes for his people. He will never have an "off day" that's been coloured by a difficult conversation; he will never speak hastily through anger. The God who cannot suffer is dependable, because he does not change. He can always help you, and his desire to help you will never wane. When you pray, he will always be ready to hear. When you fall and fail, he will be there to pick you up and to forgive. You can rest in him and rely on him. Always.

Secondly, God's complete fulfilment in every good thing means that he always has the resources to be able to help us in the face of our sufferings. In an excellent article, theologian Thomas Weinandy expresses the point well: "The compassion of God is seen then not in his suffering in solidarity with humankind, but in his ability to alleviate the cause of human suffering—sin."[29] God's unlimited resources of blessing mean that he can pour out blessing unceasingly and unstintingly. The supremely happy

---

29 Thomas Weinandy, "Does God Suffer?", *First Things*, November 2001. https://www. firstthings.com/article/2001/11/does-god-suffer (accessed 24 March 2021). I heartily recommend this article to you, along with the book of the same name.

God will one day share that happiness perfectly with his children.

Do you not know?
  Have you not heard?
The LORD is the everlasting God,
  the Creator of the ends of the earth.
He will not grow tired or weary,
  and his understanding no one can fathom.
He gives strength to the weary
  and increases the power of the weak.
Even youths grow tired and weary,
  and young men stumble and fall;
but those who hope in the LORD
  will renew their strength.
They will soar on wings like eagles;
  they will run and not grow weary,
  they will walk and not be faint. (Isaiah 40:28-31)

9. GOD CAN'T DIE

"I don't want to live forever. I mean it sounds good, but what am I going to do?" So says Bruce Willis's character Ernest Melville in the 1992 horror comedy *Death Becomes Her*. A generation later, Taylor Swift and Zayn Malik made the top 10 with a song that expresses the same sentiment: "I Don't Wanna Live Forever". Why not?

Living for ever seems, on the face of it, like a pretty desirable thing. Death is generally agreed to be a bad thing, and so that would make *not* dying a good thing. Surely it is right to "rage against the dying of the light", as the poet Dylan Thomas put it? Yet when we contemplate immortality as a real possibility, we find it is a more difficult subject that we originally imagined.

Amongst other things, there is the problem Douglas Adams alluded to in his sci-fi novel *Life, the Universe and Everything*. He describes the predicament of "Wowbagger the Infinitely Prolonged ... one of the Universe's very small number of immortal beings". Wowbagger became immortal by accident and gradually found life to be a burden:

> *In the end, it was the Sunday afternoons he couldn't cope with, and that terrible listlessness which starts to set in at about 2:55, when you know that you've had all the baths you can usefully have that day, that however hard you stare at any given paragraph in the papers you will never actually read it, or use the revolutionary new pruning technique it describes, and that as you stare at the clock the hands will move relentlessly on to four o'clock, and you will enter the long dark teatime of the soul.*[30]

Wowbagger is not the only person to have lived in dread of the long dark teatime of the soul. When I was a fresh-faced assistant minister, I remember preaching on the topic of eternal life and feeling pretty upbeat about the subject matter—that was, until one particularly insightful member of the congregation approached me and said, "The thought of eternity absolutely terrifies me". In response to my obviously rather confused expression, she said, "I'm scared that I'll be bored". She explained that if life is extended infinitely, then we will have a problem because the creation is finite. We will have time to meet every person, to have every possible

---

30 Douglas Adams, *Life, the Universe and Everything* (Macmillan, 2010), p 4-5.

conversation with every person, to read every book ever written, and to visit every interesting place until even the most thrilling destinations become commonplace and boring. By that point I had begun to experience some of her dread too. I wonder what you think I should have said to her? (Apart from, "that's a good point, I hadn't thought of that".)

Perhaps we should start by thinking about God's own immortality. That too, along with his invisibility, is part of Paul's outbursts of praise at the beginning and end of his first letter to Timothy:

> *Now to the King eternal, **immortal, invisible, the only God**, be honour and glory for ever and ever. Amen. (1 Timothy 1:17)*

> *God, the blessed and only Ruler, the King of kings and Lord of lords, **who alone is immortal**. (6:15-16)*

You see, when we talk about God as immortal, we mean something a bit different from what we normally imagine by that word. We tend to think of immortality a bit like waterproofing: you apply a certain kind of wax (or similar substance) to cloth or paper to prevent water from affecting it. So rather than me getting wet in the rain, my coat keeps the water out and it just rolls off the outside. In a similar way, we tend to think of immortality in terms of being resistant to death—a quality that can be "added" to a person who would otherwise naturally be mortal. We are far enough through the book now that you might already be ahead of me: "But you can't add anything to God". Well, quite.

As we saw in Exodus 3:14, when God chooses to reveal his name to Moses, he says "I am who I am". We noted in a previous chapter how this sets him apart from the creation as the uncreated Creator of all. He is from himself (*a se*, as you might recall) and as such everything that is true of him is part of the definition of him. Now this means that when we think about God's immortality, we are talking as much about his beginning as his end. It's not just that God can't die; it's that there is no sense in which he was "born".

Let me try to explain.

In the Septuagint, the ancient translation of the Hebrew Scriptures into the Greek language, the divine name in Exodus 3:14 is rendered as "I am the one who is" or "I am the *being one*". John, in the first chapter of Revelation, records God as saying exactly the same thing—*I am the one "who is"*—but with an important addition:

> *I am the Alpha and the Omega ... who is, and who was and who is to come, the Almighty. (Revelation 1:8)*

An almost identical phrase is then heard on the lips of the risen Jesus towards the end of the chapter:

> *I am the First and the Last. I am the **Living One**.*
> *(v 17-18)*

Notice how, in order to explain what it means for him to be "the being one" or "the living one", God describes himself in terms of the past and the future. He is a sort of bookend to reality (the "alpha and omega"[31], the "first and last"), who was and is and is to come. The whole timeline of the universe exists within these bookends; God exists outside of them.

Immortality, then, describes the mode of God's being. He is the one inevitable thing. Existing is *who* he is, not just what he does. He cannot *not* live, and he never has.

This takes us back to the idea of God existing without time. This is enormously difficult for us, because we cannot think or speak without doing so in time-bound ways— we literally cannot conceive of what eternity, unbounded by time, is like. It is just another one of those points at which we find ourselves having to say, "God just isn't like me". But when we do say that, we can begin to see ways in which life without end might not be so bad.

God, who exists outside of time and space, really is infinite in a way that things in time and space never can be. He has no end and no beginning. For that reason, no matter how long you live, you will never reach the end of *him*. The God of infinite beauty and goodness and wisdom will always have something more of himself to give you. However long you've been a Christian, you worship a God of whom there is always more to discover and more to enjoy.

---

31 The first and last letters of the Greek alphabet.

And this will be true of our lives beyond death, too. We tend to think of the blessings of the new creation solely in terms of enjoying a world that's like this one but better. When we think like that, eternity feels like an awfully long time, because the creation is finite, and our interest in and enjoyment of it will inevitably wear out. Instead, we need to shift our gaze to the Creator to whom the beauty and wonder of the world points. The highest blessing of eternal life is to know this God, who is eternal and is the giver of life. Trusting in him, you need never fear that the life to come will dissolve into the long dark teatime of the soul. Why? Because you will never get to the end of God's goodness—since you are finite, you can never reach the end of the infinite, no matter how long you've got. An infinite God is eternally captivating. Knowing this, it is possible to imagine never-ending life that is more wonderful than you ever thought possible.

You might never have lost sleep over the idea that immortality could be an unbearable burden, but some people do. Or perhaps you're someone who hates going to sleep for fear that you will never wake up. In either case, God's own immortality gives you reason for hope. Not only can he, as the Living One, offer unending life. He can make it worth living.

> Do not be afraid. I am the First and the Last. I am the Living One; I was dead, and now look, I am alive for ever and ever! And I hold the keys of death and Hades.
> (Revelation 1:17-18)

INTERLUDE 4: GOD SUFFERED AND DIED ALONE

There was an eerie quiet. It seemed almost like a blanket of calm had descended over the countryside. The hush was infectious. None of us spoke. We were sitting on a clifftop just outside the old fishing village of Mousehole at the western tip of Cornwall during a rare eclipse of the sun. We weren't quite in the path of the total eclipse (it passed us by a few miles), so it was more like late evening than the middle of the night, but even experiencing that twilight in the middle of the day was decidedly strange. It felt supernatural, even though it was a quite natural phenomenon: the moon came between the earth and the sun for a brief moment, at just the right distance to block its light. The experience did, however, put me in mind of another, much less natural event.

On the Friday of a Passover in Jerusalem nearly 2,000 years ago, darkness fell at midday. This was no eclipse—Passover was always held at a full moon, when an eclipse is impossible. But the darkness came nonetheless; for three whole hours. Yet that was not the most unnatural thing about it. Ever since, Christians have taught that the Son of God himself suffered and died in that moment of darkness. He who could not, by nature, possibly suffer, and who certainly could not die, nonetheless hung there suspended between earth and heaven, as his life drained away.

If it is a mystery that the invisible God should have appeared among us as one of us, it is a deeper mystery still that he should have disappeared in that manner. The darkness that fell in place of the hot Judean sunshine marked what was, truly, the strangest moment in the history of the universe. God died.

It became vital, amongst the Christians of the early church, to find a way of talking about this that could somehow account for its strangeness. The impossibility of this death and, yet, its reality were at the heart of God's dealings with his people. How to make sense of it? Can we really say that God *died* on the cross?

After four centuries of debate within the church, Cyril, one of the great theologians of Alexandria in Egypt (one of perhaps three cities that could claim to be the theological capital of the Christian world at the time), argued that the answer is "yes". As you might have anticipated, it comes down to the union of Christ's two natures, divine and human, in one person. Therefore, although "the Word of God is by nature immortal and incorruptible", argued Cyril, "since, however, his own body did, as Paul says, by the grace of God taste death for every man, he himself is said to have suffered death for us".[32] In other words, because it was truly his body that suffered and died, we can say that "God died" even though God, by his divine nature, cannot die.

At around the same time, the chief pastor of one of the other two cities with a claim to theological pre-eminence, Rome, made a very similar point. Jesus was fully human and fully divine "without detriment ... to the properties of either nature". And so:

For the paying off of the debt belonging to our condition, inviolable [unchangeable] nature was united with passible [subject to change, especially suffering] nature, so that, as suited the needs of our case, one

---

32 Cyril of Alexandria, "The Epistle of Cyril to Nestorius," in *A Select Library of the Nicene and Post-Nicene Fathers of the Christian Church*, Vol. 14, ed. Philip Schaff and Henry Wace, trans. Henry R. Percival, Second Series (Charles Scribner's Sons, 1900), p 198.

and the same Mediator between God and men, the Man Christ Jesus, could both die with the one and not die with the other. Thus in the whole and perfect nature of true man was true God born, complete in what was His own, complete in what was ours.[33]

That is to say: Jesus' two natures aren't joined together or mixed up with one another. Instead, they both belong to the same person, and it is that person who died and rose again for us. It is God who dies, but he dies as a man.

None of this was ivory tower theologising. The men who wrote these words were bishops in the church, responsible for the pastoral care of Christians in their own towns, and also for the teaching of the faith in the wider world. Their concern was to help God's people "to know Christ [and] the power of his resurrection and participation in his sufferings" (Philippians 3:10). A significant reason for their desire that people should know *who* died, was their conviction about *why* he died. Simply put: Jesus' death on the cross brings us salvation only because he is both fully God and fully man.

One of the classic explorations of this was provided by Athanasius, an earlier bishop of Alexandria. In his book *On the Incarnation*,

---

33 Leo the Great, "Letters," in *A Select Library of the Nicene and Post-Nicene Fathers of the Christian Church*, Vol. 12a, ed. Philip Schaff and Henry Wace, trans. Charles Lett Feltoe, Second Series (Christian Literature Company, 1895), p 40.

which is still widely available in a range of very readable translations, he discussed the problem of sin as presenting a dilemma for God.

He explained that the warning not to eat the forbidden fruit in Genesis 2:10 contains a promise: "When you eat from it you will certainly die".

When man and woman did eat that fruit...

> *What, then, was to be done? Either God must be false to His word, that for sin man must die, and let man live—which would be monstrous; or, that which had once shared in the being of the Word must sink again into non-existence through corruption—which would be unfitting. For thus God's design in creating man would be frustrated— which would be most unfitting.*[34]

Either way, it looks as though God will lose. Either he must break his word, which would be a denial of his own nature, or he must keep his promise, which will mean the destruction of humanity made in his image.

The incarnation of the Son of God ("the Word") as a man is, for Athanasius, God's elegant and beautiful solution to the problem of sin:

> *[The] Word ... for this reason takes to Himself a body capable of death,*

---

34 Athanasius of Alexandria, *Athanasius: On the Incarnation of the Word of God*, trans.

in order that it,
by being made a
partaker of the Word
who is above all,
might be a sufficient
representative of
all in the (discharge
of the penalty of)
death, and, through
the indwelling
Word, might remain
incorruptible, and
that for the future
corruption should
cease from all by
the grace of the
resurrection.

Jesus couldn't bear the consequence of our sin in death unless he was one of us; he couldn't overcome death for us unless he was God. Wonderfully for us, he was both. So what Jesus achieved by his death was nothing less than the destruction of death itself:

> *By offering to death*
> *the body He Himself*
> *took as an offering*
> *and sacrifice free*
> *from every stain, He*
> *forthwith obliterated*
> *death from all His*
> *peers by the offering of*
> *the equivalent ... For*
> *the human race had*
> *utterly perished, had*
> *not the Master and*
> *Saviour of all, the Son*
> *of God, come among*
> *us to put an end to*
> *death.*[35]

Athanasius's point was simple. God's word concerning death had to be fulfilled. Jesus died the death that was demanded in the place of his people ("His

---

T. Herbert Bindley, Second Edition Revised (The Religious Tract Society, 1903), p 23.

35 Athanasius of Alexandria, *Athanasius: On the Incarnation of the Word of God*, trans. T. Herbert Bindley, Second Edition Revised (The Religious Tract Society, 1903), p 57–58.

peers"). In so doing he was able to restore us to everlasting life—the very thing we were made for.

That is why Jesus' birth, celebrated at Christmas, along with his death, resurrection and ascension, form the heart of the Christian story. They have become for Christians the hinge around which all of history revolves. His birth marks his taking on of real humanity, his death the moment at which he bore the consequences of human rebellion, and his resurrection and ascension assure us of his victory for us, the certainty of the life he promises, and his ability to restore all things to himself.

And, in achieving all this, the God who cannot be lonely died alone. His friends and followers deserted him, and in the agonies of his death he even cried out in dereliction, "My God, my God why have you forsaken me?" (Matthew 27:46).

This shuddering moment inspired the poet Elizabeth Barrett-Browning as she reflected on the life of the great but tortured hymn writer William Cowper (1731-1800), who was plagued by the fear that he would be cut off from God and left deserted.

The final stanzas of Barrett-Browning's poem, *Cowper's Grave,* reflect on the desolation Jesus faced as he suffered on the cross. Her words offer deep comfort and courage to anyone who secretly fears that in the end they might be found unworthy of God's favour and finally be deserted by him:

*Deserted! Who hath dreamt that when the cross in
darkness rested,*
Upon the Victim's hidden face no love was manifested?
*What frantic hands outstretched have e'er the atoning
drops averted?*
*What tears have washed them from the soul, that one
should be deserted?*

*Deserted! God could separate from His own essence
rather;*
*And Adam's sins have swept between the righteous
Son and Father:*
*Yea, once, Immanuel's orphaned cry His universe hath
shaken—*
It went up single, echoless, "My God, I am forsaken!"

It went up from the Holy's lips amid His lost creation,
*That, of the lost, no son should use those words of
desolation!*
*That earth's worst phrenzies, marring hope, should
mar not hope's fruition,*
*And I, on Cowper's grave, should see his rapture in a
vision.*

The Son of God, who by nature can neither be lonely or die, became a man and died alone, so that his people would never have to face the true horror of the certain and final death that is our due. This is the extent of his love. Who, believing that, would not find rest in it?

10. GOD CAN'T BE TEMPTED

Oscar Wilde was famous for witticisms that were simultaneously so light as to appear frivolous and yet carried a hidden depth that made them rather darker than they appeared on the surface. His reported last words were: "Either this wallpaper goes or I do". Another such remark, which has made it to t-shirts around the world, is: "I can resist anything except temptation". It is a statement that could just as well serve the gleeful and arch posturing of a libertine as the anguished confession of an addict. In both scenarios, though, there is an undercurrent that suggests that, somehow, the very fact of temptation begins to relieve me of responsibility for my actions: "How could I be expected to do anything else? The temptation was just too much!"

But when we consider God, it's not just that he can *resist* temptation—by his superior will-power—it's that he isn't even tempted in the first place. And as we'll see, knowing this not only helps us to sleep easy at night, but also helps us when we are tempted.

But before we go any further, we should be clear by what we mean by "temptation". The ideas that spring to mind when we hear the word, at least if the ads I see on TV are to be believed, are probably along the line of ice-cream or sex: a powerful desire for something pleasurable but forbidden. For the observant reader of the Bible, though, temptation is a much broader and more complex concept. It is not simply about the seductive allurements of pleasure, but encompasses a whole range of testing of faith and character. The people of Israel, confronted with reports of terrifying enemies living in the promised land, were the subjects of temptation every bit as much as Joseph was when he was enticed by Potiphar's wife.

The fact that temptation can arise from all sorts of circumstances was something recognised by the writer of Proverbs, who prayed:

> ... *give me neither poverty nor riches,*
>   *but give me only my daily bread.*
> *Otherwise I may have too much and disown you*
>   *and say, "Who is the LORD?"*
> *Or I may become poor and steal*
>   *and so dishonour the name of my God.*
>
> *(Proverbs 30:8-9)*

These words acknowledge that both *having* money and *not having* money can bring temptation. They are two sides of a single coin (no pun intended). Wealth tempts me to self-reliance: *Why do I need God when I have all this money?* Poverty likewise tempts me to ignore God and rely on myself—this time, by stealing. What's striking is that the writer's understanding of himself in relation to temptation is rather like Oscar Wilde's: he knows he is prone to give in. So, he prays that he will not be led into temptation in the first place.

I'm very struck by the fact that Jesus taught his disciples to pray for just the same thing: to be given their daily bread and to be kept from temptation (Matthew 6:11-13). It's sobering to think of ourselves as so potentially helpless in the face of temptation that our best hope is to avoid it. There's no suggestion here that temptation relieves us of responsibility for our choices. There is, though, a recognition that we are frail and therefore do better, if we can, to avoid temptation than try to resist it.

It's worth looking back at the first recorded temptation as we think a bit more about why that is—and why knowing that God can't be tempted can help us when we are.

Adam and Eve were placed into a world that we can only dream of. It was a paradise with plentiful, nutritious food, full of beauty and wonder. But it was also a world with limits: there was a tree in the garden of Eden whose fruit they must not eat. But, as much as anything, those limits were an expression of what was, in fact, best about that world: it was God's world and the first people lived in it as his creatures in a relationship with him.

The temptation, when it came, was an invitation to reject the God who made them:

Now the snake was more crafty than any of the wild animals the Lord God had made. He said to the woman, "Did God really say, 'You must not eat from any tree in the garden'?"

The woman said to the serpent, "We may eat fruit from the trees in the garden, but God did say, 'You must not eat fruit from the tree that is in the middle of the garden, and you must not touch it, or you will die.'"

"You will not certainly die," the serpent said to the woman. "For God knows that when you eat from it your eyes will be opened, and you will be like God, knowing good and evil."

When the woman saw that the fruit of the tree was good for food and pleasing to the eye, and also desirable for gaining wisdom, she took some and ate it. She also gave some to her husband, who was with her, and he ate it. (Genesis 3:1-6)

Witness the progress of the conversation. First of all, the wily serpent invites Eve to doubt God's generosity: "Did God *really* say 'you must not eat from any tree in the garden'?" Although the answer to that question should have been a straight "no", Eve's actual answer shows that she bought into the idea a little bit. She adds to God's restriction in her retelling of it by saying "you must not touch it", which God hadn't said (v 3, Genesis 2:16-17).

152

From there on in, it's all downhill.

Now that negotiations have opened on what God has and hasn't said, the serpent suggests that God has been a little bit economical with the truth in his promising that the consequence of disobedience will be death: "You will not certainly die," the serpent assures her. In fact, he suggests, God has only imposed restrictions on Adam and Eve in order to limit them and protect his unique position. That is, *God wants to keep the best things from you and hold them for himself.*

Bear in mind what has happened in the story so far. The Universe has come into being, and taken on a certain shape, all by means of God's word. He spoke and it happened. There is only one word that has not yet come to pass, and it's the word about death if they eat the fruit. So, this is the decisive moment: will they believe God's word or believe the speculative serpent who suggests that God's word is not so powerful as all that? That suggestion that God's word might *not* be fulfilled is no mere quibble over language choice. It casts doubt on God's unique status as creator, his "Godness" if you like. What's more, in suggesting that God is concerned for himself and not his creatures, the serpent calls into question God's goodness as well.

That combination of doubting God's goodness and his "Godness" is remarkably helpful in understanding how temptation works on our hearts. Think, for instance, about the temptation to lie. For me, I am most tempted to lie to other people when I feel that the truth will cause them to think badly of me. Let's say I am late for a meeting. Rather than leaving people to conclude that I am either disorganised or disrespectful, I find myself desperately fighting the urge to invent traffic on the route or some emergency that meant I couldn't leave the house in a timely fashion. What's going on there?

In one sense, wanting to be well thought of is natural and good. The writer of Proverbs says that "a good name is more desirable than great riches" (Proverbs 22:1). But when that desire is so strong that I am willing to break one of the Ten Commandments to get it, then there's something very wrong.

It comes down to that question of how I think about God. If I really think that it would be worse if people know the truth about me (that is, that I don't always value punctuality as much as I should in my cultural context, thus demonstrating my lack of love and concern for others), than that I should treat God with contempt (which is what breaking his clear command does), then it seems likely that I believe that other people's opinions are more important than God to me. As such, I am tempted because I don't really think of God as being truly supreme—I doubt his "Godness".

In other situations, there may be something that God's word forbids me, that I feel I really need in order to flourish and be fulfilled. If I doubt God's goodness in putting that thing off limits, the temptation will be unbearable. How many extra-marital affairs have begun with the justification that somehow this relationship will make the participants feel "whole"?

So, all temptation has its roots in doubting either God's Godness or his goodness (and frequently, both). In light of this, it begins to become clear why God cannot be tempted. It might help you to think of it like this. We used to care sometimes for a friend's dog, who was growing so fast that the vet had told his owners to keep him on a highly restricted diet. If he was allowed to eat as much as his growing body wanted, he would develop serious problems with his skeleton and would be permanently plagued by dislocating bones and chronic pain. As a result of his medically restricted diet, this poor creature was permanently hungry. On walks we had to be incredibly vigilant, because he was so ravenous that even cowpats were an irresistible temptation. While I know what it is to be tempted, what this poor beast found irresistible was never a temptation to me. Instead, it was utterly revolting.

To God, anything we might see as a temptation is like that. Anything that is contrary to his inherent goodness is disgusting. After all, what motivation could God have to treat something else as more supreme than himself? We are tempted when we doubt God's "Godness" and put other things in his place. Do we really think that God might doubt himself? Similarly, what good thing does God lack that he might be tempted to seek by illegitimate means? For God to be tempted by evil he would have to reject his own existence. For that reason, we should be able to agree that God can no more cease to be good than he can cease to be.

Perhaps you can see how that helps us, too. Knowing that God cannot be tempted is another way of saying that he is always and unalterably good. And, given that many of our own temptations have their roots in doubting God's goodness, thinking about God's relationship to temptation might be a real help with that.

This was the case for a group of struggling Christians to whom Jesus's (half) brother James addressed his book. The readers of James's letter were suffering. Their faith was being tested severely by persecution and hardship, and James recognised the danger that posed. They could be tempted to believe that age-old lie about God: the lie that he doesn't love his people. So having explained the source of temptation and warned against its effects (1:13-15), James immediately goes on to say:

> [16] *Don't be deceived, my dear brothers and sisters.* [17] *Every good and perfect gift is from above, coming down from the Father of the heavenly lights, who does not change like shifting shadows.* [18] *He chose to give us birth through the word of truth, that we might be a kind of firstfruits of all he created. (James 1:16-18)*

Humans have tended to view their fortunes as constantly subject to change. Frequently they have put this fact together with the changes they observe all around them in the creation—one of the most enduring myths that humans have been subject to is that of astrology, the idea that somehow our destinies are shaped by the movements of the sun, moon, stars and planets. In one sense, of course, this is true. Such motions change the weather and the seasons. But God is not like those heavenly bodies which shift and change (v 17). His relationship to his people is not subject to seasons or changes in the weather. He is wonderfully constant, and constantly good.

God doesn't change, says James, *and if he has brought you to new life, it isn't probationary*. God is not in the business of seeing how hard he can push you to see whether you fail. For that reason, we do not need to view temptation with the same grim determinism as Oscar Wilde did. Temptation does not have the irresistible power of God behind it. Nor is it a sign that God is out to get you. Knowing that God is unstintingly *for* his people is a great help in resisting temptation, because temptation relies in one way or another on the lie that he is not. "God loves me, and going his way is the path of blessing" is a great thing to say to yourself when your circumstances, whether they play on your desires or your fears, entice you to believe otherwise. In what situation might you need to remember that?

Furthermore, we can sleep at night, as Paul puts it, "being confident of this, that he who began a good work in you will carry it on to completion until the day of Christ Jesus" (Philippians 1:6). God always has been and always will be unchangeably good. We can trust him. No matter what the weather or the season, whatever our circumstances, he hasn't changed and his promises remain secure. In such knowledge, we can rest.

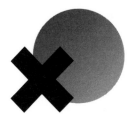

11. GOD CAN'T LIE

There is something in the art of the comic that allows them to wield a prophetic sword in a world that doesn't like to hear the truth about itself. So, it has been from time immemorial. The jester could say things in the presence of a medieval king that would have anyone else languishing in a dungeon awaiting the scaffold.

This ability is one of the things I love about the comedian and writer Ricky Gervais. Albeit through a carefully constructed persona, he is willing to say things that are uncomfortable, and to give voice to unwelcome truths. That was one reason why I was very keen to see the film he wrote and directed, *The Invention of Lying*, when it hit cinemas a few years back.

The film takes place in an alternative reality in which everyone tells the truth, all the time. It begins with an imaginative retelling of the first time someone told a lie, and it then invites the viewer to consider what the world would be like if that had never happened.

A world without lying would be a world without dreams. A world without pretence. A world without fiction. A world without flattery. A world very unlike our own.

The film then features a series of toe curling-encounters between people who simply say exactly what they are thinking about each other. The film's hero Mark, played by Ricky Gervais, is told in an early scene by the woman he is pursuing romantically that he has no chance, because although he is funny and nice to be with...

... none of that changes the fact that you'd still be contributing half of the genetic code to our children. I don't want short, fat kids with little snub noses.

I'll be honest(!), I don't find that aspect of the film particularly convincing—surely there is a difference between being truthful and saying exactly what goes through your mind without concern for the consequences to yourself or others. But it is a device that plays well for laughs and allows Ricky Gervais to prick the bubbles of lots of the little hypocrisies and dishonesties of everyday life. The plot itself centres around the fact that Mark is the only man in the world with the ability to lie. But hidden behind this conceit there is a much more subtle and nuanced idea in play.

The characters in the film do not have the vocabulary to describe the act of telling a lie. So, when Mark sees the anguish on his dying mother's face and tries to comfort her by saying that she's not going to an eternity of nothingness, but to a mansion in the sky, the only way he can reflect on it with his friends is to say, "I said something... that wasn't".

In the prologue to the movie, the ability to lie is described as leading to...

> ... *the birth of imagination itself, story-telling, religion, and the oh-so-important polite lie, as in, "Oh Patty, have you lost weight? You look fantastic."*

In other words, the film invites us to consider untruth as fundamental to creativity and culture: to the capacity to think in new ways and to relate positively to others. And before you reject that thought out of hand, it is worth asking what creativity is, if not the ability to imagine and express something that isn't.

The film may be lightweight, but its writer and director is not. He took a degree in philosophy and has acquitted himself well in debate with Rowan Williams, the former Archbishop of Canterbury, himself an internationally renowned academic and intellectual. Ricky Gervais is an atheist, and a very persuasive one. In this film, he treats belief in God as something impossible without the uniquely human ability to subvert truth in order to exert power over ourselves or others. Belief in God, he suggests, is a kind of soothing self-deceit. There's nothing new in that idea. But what is new here, to me at least, is the idea that the capacity to lie is essential to creativity. And if that is the case, belief in a God of truth as Creator is absurd.

So, are we right to insist that our creator God cannot lie? The Bible certainly does. The God of Abraham, Isaac and Jacob is the God of truth: "The LORD detests lying lips, but he delights in people who are trustworthy" (Proverbs 12:22). In the New Testament, his truthfulness is essential to his being. In John's Gospel, Jesus says of himself that he is "the truth" (John 14:6); he describes the Holy Spirit as "the Spirit of truth" (14:17; 15:26; 16:13); and says of the Father that he can only be worshipped in truth (4:23). Jesus also says that the Spirit of truth goes out from the Father (15:26), that the Father's word is truth (17:17), and that he sent Jesus into the world to testify to the truth (18:37). In the epistles we read that "God ... does not lie" (Titus 1:2), that it is "impossible for God to lie" (Hebrews 6:18), and that he alone is uniquely truthful—"let God be true and every human being a liar" (Romans 3:4).

But if we take the Ricky Gervais definition of lying as "saying something that isn't", then God's inability to lie is called into question. Because the very first chapter of the Bible features little other than God saying things that aren't. He speaks of light when there has only ever been darkness; he speaks of life when there has only ever been emptiness. God has this creative capacity to imagine and say things that do not correspond to the existing reality.

Is that a lie? Well, the writer of Genesis did not seem to think so, because he is at pains to point out that every time God said something, reality was in a hurry to conform itself to the word God had spoken. "Let there be light," says God, "and there was light," replies the newly minted universe. Far from God's creativity being a challenge to his truthfulness, it is instead a demonstration of its power. Just as we saw with knowledge—he knows what is true by creating—so with his truthfulness. The normal order is reversed. When I speak, my words are true if they conform to reality. When God speaks, his words are true because reality must follow.

It would be easy to be misled by this line of argument though. And in the Middle Ages, for instance, theologians and philosophers like William of Ockham[36] almost went so far as to suggest that God's goodness (and within that, his truthfulness) were simply expressions of his power. So, there were those who insisted that if God suddenly decided that torturing kittens was a good thing, then it would become a good thing. (Well, they might not have put it in exactly those terms, but that was the gist of it.)

This is all related to the previous chapter, the idea that God cannot be tempted by evil, and it comes down to an ancient problem posed by the philosopher Plato.[37] The question can be put like this: "Is the good good because

---

36 Famed for "Ockham's Razor", which is often summarised as, "The simplest explanation is the best one".

37 His dialogue Euthyphro is considered foundational in this area.

God wills it or does God will the good because it is good?".
In other words, is there a standard outside God to which
he conforms, or is it all just arbitrary (that is: a matter of
will)?[38] Even though the question seems to be a dilemma
(that is, that either one or other option must be true),
neither of these options quite work to describe God's
relationship to the true and the good.

Instead, we must say that both are simultaneously true,
but only when held together. God wills the good because
it is good and it is good because he wills it. This is because
God's own being is the definition of goodness. He is the
yardstick against which every claim to goodness or truth is
measured. He cannot even be tempted to do evil, because
his own goodness prevents it. He cannot lie, because he is
truth, and so everything he does is in accordance with the
truth and all that is true derives from him.

The real flaw in the logic of *The Invention of Lying* is to see
the roots of creativity and imagination in the capacity to
lie. It is true that a person cannot lie if they do not have
the ability to imagine things that aren't. In that sense
there is a relationship between the two. But it is not the
capacity to lie that is essential to creation; it is the capacity
to create that is essential to lying. Lying comes from a
misuse of an otherwise good faculty.

This is in fact true of every kind of evil. Take the area of sex
as an example. Sex is good. The human drive to reproduce

---

38 The Latin word that we translate as will (i.e. the faculty of will) is *arbitrio*.

reflects the very first commandment given to humanity: *Go forth and multiply* (Genesis 1:28). The "one flesh" union of Adam and Eve was part of the quintessential goodness of the pre-fall world. But that capacity for attraction and connection, present in the sexual impulse, can so easily be used for evil. There is more evidence of that in pretty much any day's news cycle than there is in the whole of the Bible. The percentage of women who have suffered some sort of sexual assault, for example, is staggering and appalling. All sin involves, in one way or another, a twisting or a denial of something good.

So it is with the lie. The ability to speak is good. The capacity for creation and imagination is good. Indeed, both these things are reflections of God's character. But these things can be twisted to evil ends.

As we saw in the previous chapter, the world was doomed by a lie. The lie is fundamentally an act of violence. Jesus says that "the devil ... was a murderer from the beginning, not holding to the truth, for there is no truth in him. When he lies, he speaks his native language, for he is a liar and the father of lies" (John 8:44). It is very intriguing to see lies and murder put together in this way. But when we remember that all of reality is established by God's truthful speech, it makes sense that any attempt to subvert that reality by untruthful speech should be seen as fundamentally destructive.

So, when we learn that God cannot lie, what we are observing once again is his goodness. He will not lie for the same reason that he will not judge unjustly or try to trick or tempt you into failure. His truthfulness is both a mark and an expression of his character as the generous giver of life and all good things. The whole story of the world begins by giving life and beauty and bounty to his creatures. He does all this by speaking.

God's inability to lie is of real personal significance to us. Consider again Hebrews 6:18, where we are told that it is impossible for God to lie. What's striking is the context. The writer is talking about the incident in the Old Testament when God promised to bless Abraham and his descendants, which by faith includes us. Here is how we can know that God will deliver on that promise:

People swear by someone greater than themselves, and the oath confirms what is said and puts an end to all argument. Because God wanted to make the unchanging nature of his purpose very clear to the heirs of what was promised, he confirmed it with an oath. God did this so that, by two unchangeable things in which it is impossible for God to lie, we who have fled to take hold of the hope set before us may be greatly encouraged. We have this hope as an anchor for the soul, firm and secure. It enters the inner sanctuary behind the curtain, where our forerunner, Jesus, has entered on our behalf. (v 16-20)

Let that sink in. God has made an unchangeable, unshakeable promise that we can build our lives on. Some people feel that a promise must be a pretty insecure foundation to base everything on. After all, how can you be sure a promise will be kept? But if the God who cannot lie has gone so far as to swear an oath on himself to secure that promise, then there is nothing firmer or more real imaginable. God swearing an oath on himself is the most wonderful virtuous circle. His word is already infinitely trustworthy, but he wants us to be so secure in his promise that he multiplies infinity by infinity, and says, *You can trust me this much.*

The writer to the Hebrews invites us to think about God's promises of salvation as an anchor for the soul. Imagine it like the tether that keeps an astronaut attached to a spacecraft when they go on a "space walk". As long as that tether is there, they have a way home. Even though they are in the vastness of space, where there is nothing to hold on to, nothing to push against, nothing that could get them back to safety, with that connection they are safe and will not be lost.

The same is true of God's promises. Even if every other certainty in your life collapses, you have this connection to safety—this anchor that keeps you connected to him. No global pandemic, climate crisis or failure of the economy can cut you loose from that. Nor can the collapse of a relationship, the loss of your reputation or a failure at work or school send you spinning off into space. God's promises in Jesus will not fail.

Everyone will one day go into the deep dark void that is the grave. All of us will enter eternity and face whatever lies the other side. That God has provided an anchor in the most glorious place imaginable—his own presence—means that you can rest in peace, even now, because your future peace is certain. God has promised it, so reality is bound to conform—because God cannot lie. Where Jesus is, you will be too.

INTERLUDE 5: JESUS WAS TEMPTED

The comedian Steve Martin once said, "Before you criticize a man, walk a mile in his shoes. That way, when you do criticise him, you'll be a mile away and have his shoes." It's a classic comedic move—twisting a cliché piece of advice to reveal its hidden absurdity. But though clichés are vulnerable to this treatment, they only become clichés because they contain enough truth to be widely repeated.

The idea of walking a mile in another person's shoes is a way of reminding us that we cannot really interpret someone else's life decisions without understanding their situation and experience from the inside. In an ultimate sense, of course, that is impossible—we can never truly know what it is like to be another person.[39] But we can often draw on experiences and feelings that can help us to understand what someone else is going through, even though we could never accurately claim to "know exactly how you feel".

When it comes to human experience, and perhaps especially the experience of temptation, we would naturally expect God to be at a loss. How could he possibly understand? And it is here that we find another huge surprise in the life of Jesus, placed prominently in the Gospel narratives of Jesus' life. So prominent is the account of Jesus' temptation, in fact, that on one occasion when a friend at university invited me to try drugs, and realised that my reluctance stemmed from my Christian faith, they followed it up by playfully paraphrasing the words of Satan to Jesus: "Go on... all the kingdoms of the world..."

The writer to the Hebrews makes much of the significance of Jesus' temptations as being on our behalf. In Hebrews 2, the writer tells us that "because [Jesus] himself suffered when he was tempted, he is able to help those who are being tempted" (Hebrews 2:18). And in Hebrews 4 we're assured that Jesus is able "to

---

39 By the way, if you want to explore that particular question further, then I can do nothing better than recommend that you read the philosopher Thomas Nagel's seminal essay, "What is it like to be a bat?". Thomas Nagel, "What is it like to be a bat?" *The Philosophical Review*, Vol. 83, No. 4 (October, 1974), p 435-450.

feel sympathy for our weaknesses" because he "has been tempted in every way, just as we are—yet he did not sin" (4:15).

Reflect on that for a moment—Jesus can empathise with us when we are tempted, because he too has been tempted. We will come back to these verses later, but for now, let it sink in that the Son of God, who by nature can never be tempted, actually understands our temptations from the inside.

At this point, if you feel at all like Oscar Wilde (who, you'll remember from chapter 10, was able to resist anything expect temptation), you might be thinking: "Yes, but Jesus doesn't *really* understand because he never gave in". But that response actually misses the strength of what the writer to the Hebrews is saying. He wants us to understand that Jesus' experience of temptation was in fact *more* complete than ours, because he never gave in.

Think about it like this. The other day, I had to take my day off when the rest of the family were all busy at school or at work. (I'm a minister, so the hours are somewhat irregular.) Alone and with nothing else to do, it seemed like a good idea to set out on a 70-mile bike ride. To the seasoned road cyclist this would be no great achievement, but I hadn't sat on a bike at all for several months. It was, in many ways, an act of utter stupidity. That is certainly what my body began to tell me after about 35 miles of riding through the beautiful English countryside. The temptation to quit and find a train station and beg to be allowed, sweaty and disgusting though I was, to board a train with my bike, was almost unbearable. How could I go on? I began to feel slightly unhinged and even sang a duet with my legs—in which they pointed out some home truths about the benefit of graduated programmes of exercise! In the end I pressed on and somehow made it home—albeit in a bit of a state.

Would I have known more about the temptation to quit if I had given up? No! I would have known more about giving in to it. But the full power of the temptation could only be experienced by carrying on. It got worse with every mile. I had to endure it all the way to the end to really understand everything it had to throw at me. Notice that Jesus *"suffered* when he was tempted" (Hebrews 2:18). Jesus faced the full might of temptation's power by resisting it. In that sense, he knows more about temptation than Oscar Wilde, or, for that matter, any of us.

And what was the temptation that Jesus faced? In Matthew 4:1-11, the passage my young university friend was referring to, we're shown that Jesus' experience was typical of the temptation faced by God's people in the Old Testament. Out in the wilderness, Jesus was confronted by the devil, who tried the same tack that worked both with Adam in the Garden of Eden, and the children of Israel in the desert en route to the promised land. Satan tried to tempt Jesus to disobedience using food.

Then Jesus was led by the Spirit into the wilderness to be tempted by the devil. After fasting forty days and forty nights, he was hungry. The tempter came to him and said, "If you are the Son of God, tell these stones to become bread." (v 1-3)

Jesus, though, recognised what was really at stake. He answered, "It is written: 'Man shall not live on bread alone, but on every word that comes from the mouth of God'" (v 4).

And having succeeded where Adam failed, Jesus pressed on into as-yet untested depths of temptation.

Then the devil took him to the holy city and had him stand on the highest point of the temple. "If you are the Son of God," he said, "throw yourself down. For it is written:

"'He will command his angels concerning you, and they will lift you up in their hands, so that you will not strike your foot against a stone.'"

Jesus answered him, "It is also written: 'Do not put the Lord your God to the test.'"

Again, the devil took him to a very high mountain and showed him all the kingdoms of the world and their splendor. "All this I will give you," he said, "if you will bow down and worship me."

Jesus said to him, "Away from me, Satan! For it is written:

> *"'Worship the Lord your God, and serve him only.'"*
>
> *Then the devil left him, and angels came and attended him.*
>
> *(v 5-11)*

We don't have space here for a detailed exploration of this extraordinary account from Matthew. But I would like to draw your attention to one thing that helps to make sense of how Jesus "suffered when he was tempted" and how, ultimately, he can help people like us.

The climax of the temptation is the offer of all worldly power. This is a power that we know Jesus was concerned with. Indeed, he has since received it. Paul writes to the Philippians that "God exalted him to the highest place and gave him the name that is above every name, that at the name of Jesus every knee should bow, in heaven and on earth and under the earth, and every tongue acknowledge that Jesus Christ is Lord" (Philippians 2:9-11).

The temptation here is not so much *what* is on offer as the *route* Jesus is invited to take. Satan's offer is of a quick and painless route to glory. The God-ordained journey before Jesus, though, was of a different sort.

The sentence from Philippians quoted above actually begins with the word "therefore". The verses before it give the reason for Jesus' exaltation. What is it?

> *[Jesus], being in very nature God, did not consider equality with God something*

to be used to his own advantage; rather, he made himself nothing by taking the very nature of a servant, being made in human likeness. And being found in appearance as a man, he humbled himself by becoming obedient to death— even death on a cross!

(v 6-8)

On the high mountain with Satan, Jesus was offered a kingdom without a cross. Thankfully, he chose the cross.

That is the heart of Jesus' temptation. He suffered when he was tempted, because, in the end, the greatest temptation was not to suffer. To quote Hebrews 2 again at slightly more length:

For this reason he had to be made like them, fully human in every way, in order that he might become a merciful and faithful high priest in service to God, and that he might make atonement for the sins of the people. Because he himself suffered when he was tempted, he is able to help those who are being tempted.

(Hebrews 2:17-18)

In the end, Jesus is able to help us not just as an example, or someone who can empathise, but as a Saviour. He resisted temptation all the way to the end, so that he could put right what we as a human race have got wrong.

Irenaeus, Bishop of Lyons, whose own mentor had been personally acquainted with the apostle John, wrote this about Jesus' temptation:

> *The trespass which came by the tree was undone by the tree of obedience, when, hearkening unto God, the Son of man was nailed to the tree … By the obedience wherewith He obeyed even unto death, hanging on the tree, He put away the old disobedience which was wrought in the tree.*[40]

Jesus faced up to the worst possible temptation in order to remake a world that was otherwise irreparably broken by sin. Jesus endured to the very end by fixing his eyes on the goal of eternity with us. As the writer to the Hebrews says, "For the joy that was set before him he endured the cross, scorning its shame, and sat down at the right hand of the throne of God" (12:2).

So, when you're tempted, and you know you're being tempted—whether that's in something big, like abandoning your faith, or comparatively small, like "accidentally" leaving something off your tax return[41]—here's what you can do. First, you can pray, knowing that God really *does* understand what you're going through. You can remember that Jesus knows exactly how much more it might hurt if you

---

40 Irenaeus of Lyons, *The Demonstration of the Apostolic Preaching*, trans. J. Armitage Robinson, D.D. (SPCK, 1920), p 100-101.

41 I would wish at this point to stress that I do not want to encourage a *laissez-faire* approach to tax fraud, but just to offer an example of the sorts of things that might easily slip by some people's consciences!

resist. But most of all, you can recognise that when faced with much more painful temptation than anything you or I have ever experienced, Jesus chose to go through the pain to get to you. Whatever reward temptation may offer, a God who loves you like that is worth infinitely more.

12. GOD CAN'T DISOWN HIMSELF

If, like me, you enjoy reading and watching spy thrillers, you might be familiar with the concept of a "burn notice". Essentially, if an undercover agent is considered to have become unreliable, or if there is a danger that their actions will cause embarrassment to the government, then they can be disavowed. What that basically means is that they are cut loose. They no longer belong to or represent the government or agency that employed them. They are on their own. Not only is the "burn notice" a great device in fiction—it's part of the basis for the *Mission Impossible* films and lots of other books and shows—it is also, apparently, something that can happen for real.

That idea of disavowal is what this last chapter is about. When we read in Paul's second letter to Timothy that

"[God] cannot disown himself" (2 Timothy 2:13), it's talking about that sort of rejection or denial. The point is that God cannot issue a burn notice against himself. While that may seem quite obvious, it's actually quite a helpful recap of what the other eleven things God can't do have taught us about who he is. More than that, though, it is a great way to see how all these things really can help you to sleep at night.

We've seen that God is the only necessary being. He exists because of who he is ("I AM WHO I AM"). He is the Living One—he cannot die. And he is perfect—there is nothing about him that could be better, and there is nothing missing. It makes sense, then, that a God like this cannot deny himself. He is the one truly undeniable reality, and everything else that exists only does so because of him. To deny himself would be to dissolve all of reality.

But that's not going to happen. It can't. The God who cannot learn, because all knowledge already belongs to him, could hardly be expected to act as if the most true thing (himself) was untrue. The God who cannot be surprised will never encounter some new thing that could cause him to rethink his view of himself. Even if he did, he can't change his mind anyway, because there is nothing that could cause it to change.

The God who is invisible, because he doesn't have a body but lives beyond our universe, is not going to develop some kind of hormonal or chemical imbalance and turn away from or against himself. The God whose eyes are too

pure to look on evil is not going reject his own goodness—
since that is itself the heart of evil.

I guess you get the point. God must and always will
remain entirely true to himself, because there is no other
way for him to be. That is supremely good news, of course,
because it means that whatever else may happen in this
world of chance and change, there is a deeper reality that
remains stable and trustworthy. Although it often feels
as though the universe is pitiless and cold, the God who
stands behind it is unchangeably strong and kind. So we
can have confidence that every wrong will be put right
in the end, and that truth will be vindicated despite the
tapestry of lies that enshrouds much of human life.

But that's the big picture. And I live, by comparison, in a
very small part of a very small picture. Does this actually
mean anything for me and my life?

Paul's statement that God "cannot disown himself" forms
part of a "trustworthy saying"—a type of memorable
snippet that Paul sometimes recounts in his letters. Enjoy
it in full:

> [11] *Here is a trustworthy saying:*
>   *If we died with him,*
>   *we will also live with him;*
> [12] *if we endure,*
>   *we will also reign with him.*
>   *If we disown him,*
>   *he will also disown us;*

> [13] *if we are faithless,*
>   *he remains faithful,*
>   *for he cannot disown himself.*
>
> *(2 Timothy 2:11-13)*

Paul's "trustworthy saying" is an encouragement to hold tight—to keep trusting Jesus—even at those times when the world seems to be trying to force us to let go. In fact, at the time Paul was writing he was under great pressure to abandon his faith. He was in prison for preaching about Jesus and many of his friends had disavowed him, because he was dangerous to know. So, when he says, "If we died with him, we will also live with him; if we endure, we will also reign with him" (v 11-12), that's no ivory-tower theology lesson. That is a life-or-death reminder that no one can take away what Jesus has won for his people.

And as we've seen, Jesus won it at great cost to himself. The invisible God became visible. The God who cannot learn went to school. The God who cannot be tempted endured temptation. The God who can never be lonely cried out in desolation and the Living One died. He did all that to give us life instead of death, to restore our broken relationship with God, and to remake us as we were meant to be. *So*, says Paul, *hold on!*

The alternative is terrible: "If we disown him, he will also disown us" (v 12). The Christian who issues a burn notice against Jesus—who considers him dangerous to know and joins his enemies—cuts themselves off from their only hope. I can only imagine the anguish with which Paul considered that prospect.

Maybe you aren't quite tempted to disown him in that way at the moment, but you feel like you are hanging by a thread. Perhaps the Christian life has felt hard for you for some time. You are weary and, to be honest, you aren't sure if you've got enough in the tank to make it to the end. Will your faith be strong enough? You have no problem believing all the things we've been reminded of about God in this book, but it doesn't help you sleep, because you fear that you might be losing your grip on him.

To someone like that, Paul's last phrase in this "trustworthy saying" is worth more than finding Elon Musk's online banking password: "If we are faithless, he remains faithful, for he cannot disown himself" (v 13). Did you get that? Even if we are faithless—even if our faith is weak and pathetic, to the point that it hardly seems up to the job—God will hold true to the promises he made us. He has committed himself to us to the extent that disowning you, even if your faith is hanging by a thread, would be like disowning himself. And as we've seen, that isn't going to happen. "If we are faithless, he remains faithful for he cannot disown himself."

In the last chapter we reflected on a passage that says that God, in making his covenant promises to his people, "swore by himself" (Hebrews 6:13). It's as if he was in a court of law, but instead of a Bible, God swore his promises to his people on his own being. God has sworn by himself.

He cannot disown himself. He will not abandon you, or let you fall. You could never rest safely in your own strength or faithfulness. But you can rest in his. So sleep well!

ACKNOWLEDGEMENTS

My grateful thanks to Rachel Jones at The Good Book Company, who has been the most gracious and insightful editor a writer could hope for; to the many kind friends (I trust you know who you are!) who have encouraged me along the way; to the church family at St Bartholomew's Edgbaston; and most of all to Sam, Miriam, Harriet and Oliver: "Team Tucker". S.D.G.

thegoodbook
COMPANY

BIBLICAL | RELEVANT | ACCESSIBLE

At The Good Book Company, we are dedicated to helping Christians and local churches grow. We believe that God's growth process always starts with hearing clearly what he has said to us through his timeless word—the Bible.

Ever since we opened our doors in 1991, we have been striving to produce Bible-based resources that bring glory to God. We have grown to become an international provider of user-friendly resources to the Christian community, with believers of all backgrounds and denominations using our books, Bible studies, devotionals, evangelistic resources, and DVD-based courses.

We want to equip ordinary Christians to live for Christ day by day, and churches to grow in their knowledge of God, their love for one another, and the effectiveness of their outreach.

Call us for a discussion of your needs or visit one of our local websites for more information on the resources and services we provide.

Your friends at The Good Book Company

thegoodbook.com | thegoodbook.co.uk
thegoodbook.com.au | thegoodbook.co.nz
thegoodbook.co.in